A Heavy Yoke

For those who have survived, those who have not, and those who have only in part.

A Heavy Yoke

*Theology, Power and Abuse
in the Church*

Selina Stone

scm press

© Selina Stone 2025

Published in 2025 by SCM Press

Editorial office
3rd Floor, Invicta House,
110 Golden Lane,
London EC1Y 0TG, UK
www.scmpress.co.uk

SCM Press is an imprint of Hymns Ancient & Modern Ltd
(a registered charity)

Hymns Ancient & Modern

Hymns Ancient & Modern® is a registered trademark of
Hymns Ancient & Modern Ltd
13A Hellesdon Park Road, Norwich,
Norfolk NR6 5DR, UK

All rights reserved. No part of this publication may be reproduced,
stored in a retrieval system, or transmitted,
in any form or by any means, electronic, mechanical,
photocopying or otherwise, without the prior permission of
the publisher, SCM Press.

The Author has asserted their right under the Copyright, Designs and
Patents Act 1988 to be identified as the Author of this Work

British Library Cataloguing in Publication data

A catalogue record for this book is available
from the British Library

Scripture quotations, unless otherwise stated, are taken from The Holy Bible,
New International Version (Anglicised edition) copyright © 1979, 1984, 2011
by Biblica (formerly International Bible Society). Used by permission of Hodder
& Stoughton Publishers, an Hachette UK company. All rights reserved.

Scripture quotations marked (NRSV) are from New Revised Standard Version
Bible: Anglicized Edition, copyright © 1989, 1995 National Council of the
Churches of Christ in the United States of America. Used by permission.
All rights reserved worldwide.

Scripture quotations marked (NKJV) are taken from the New King James
Version®. Copyright © 1982 by Thomas Nelson. Used by permission.
All rights reserved.

ISBN: 978-0-334-06669-9

EU GPSR Authorised Representative
LOGOS EUROPE, 9 rue Nicolas Poussin, 17000, LA ROCHELLE, France
E-mail: Contact@logoseurope.eu

No part of this book may be used or reproduced in any manner for the
purpose of training artificial intelligence technologies or systems.

Typeset by Regent Typesetting

Contents

Foreword vii
Introduction 1

1 Power and Theology 15
2 Words from God? Calling, Power and Speech 33
3 The Almighty: Power, Our Work and God's Ways 53
4 On Principalities and Powers 73
5 Sanctifying Suffering: The Cross and Christian Abuse 90
6 The Problem of Vulnerability 109
7 The Power of Discernment 131

Bibliography 154
Index of Names and Subjects 159

Foreword

'I lost myself, my faith and my God in the experience, power was revered and misused over and over and yet no one ever preaches about this.' These words, written by someone who has experienced spiritual abuse, are stark and honest. The misuse of power is so integral to the experience of spiritual abuse. In the past years, revelations of abuses of power and experiences of abuse in religious contexts have been sadly regular occurrences. For victim-survivors the impact and longevity of these experiences cannot be underestimated. The testimonies of those who have experienced harm have rightly called for acknowledgement, response, justice and prevention. In seeking to address abuses of power, there have been a number of helpful texts approaching this topic from different lenses and perspectives. However, it has often been said to me that what is missing is the theology. There is a need to grapple with and explore theological perspectives on power and how these are related to experiences of abuse. Without this our understanding is like a jigsaw with missing pieces – we cannot see the whole and therefore we cannot address it fully.

This book, which seeks to explore how power works in and through theology and how this power can be abused, is both timely and important. It is written from Selina Stone's position as a Christian theologian committed to encouraging us to consider how our Christian beliefs and spiritual habits shape how we live. Therefore, for those who are theologians it is a deeply important book to read and reflect on, offering new and fresh perspectives and challenges. One of the key elements of the book is that it allows a gateway for those of us who are not theologians to begin to explore not only the connection between theology and power, but also our own theologies that we operate out of and may not be aware of. I have had people reflect on my own work on spiritual abuse and ask the question, 'But you are not a theologian, are you?' It is indeed true that I am not, and the message behind the comment is to suggest that without being a theologian the work is undermined. While I do not agree with this and think that we need many different approaches to understanding abuses of power and that the testimonies of victim-survivors speak powerfully, I have for many years stated that understanding theology is important. As I say, it provides pieces to the jigsaw which are essential. However, as a non-theologian, I have often found trying to 'crack open the door of theology' a difficult task. Theological texts are often written seemingly for theologians and therefore can hold the door firmly shut to those without the tools to access and make sense of the language being used. This book is refreshing in that it actively seeks to be accessible, written in a way that encourages and invites those of us without a theological background to the table and in so doing not only educates but also challenges us and allows us to explore our own theologies. While the book rightly explores abuse of power and takes time to explore this in depth, it also comes from a position of hope that we can do and be better.

This is not a book that seeks to give a blanket overall view on theology and power, rather it is honest and authentic in exploring the many nuances of power and how it operates. Power is messy, it is not held equally by all, and our Christian assumptions of power are often not based in theology or world reality. This book shines a light on some of the complexity and inequality in experiences of living as a Christian within Christian communities. It goes beyond a theological journey into power and challenges some deep-rooted inequities in the way in which we value and treat others. It motivates us to reflect deeply and meaningfully on how we think and behave and how power is inherent for some people because of what we have valued and privileged. It requires us to ask questions about our assumptions and the ways in which we have developed power structures in our communities. It calls us to reflect on differences between what we say and what we embody or show in our actions and conversations, structures and institutions.

The book begins with setting the scene and helping us understand why the book is needed and what it seeks to do. It covers where and how power is held and the relationship between theology and power. It calls us to reflect on language, beliefs, cultures and thinking. It requires us to think about the language we use, the voices we silence, our measurements of 'success' in ministry, our understandings of unity, sacrifice and suffering, vulnerability and discernment. It suggests that we rarely honestly explore or examine God's power. Through reflection on cases of abuse, Selina Stone explores and explains how power is inherent, maintained and employed.

I think one of the most engaging things about this book is that it causes a reaction; there are times at which you read it and think, 'Yes! How did I not see that before?' There are times in which the book reinforces and expands your thinking and many times where it challenges. There will also be times where you disagree and that is important. Selina Stone is inviting us into her rigorously researched and developed arguments but also encouraging our autonomy. The book makes us ask repeatedly, 'What do I think about that?' or 'That makes me uncomfortable, but why?' The purpose of the book is not to provide all the answers but to provide tools so we can reflect and consider what our answers are and importantly where those answers come from and through this move forward to a clearer understanding of how power operates in and through theology. The book has the potential to change how we think and how we act and to facilitate us to ask questions about the dynamics of power in churches, which may result in greater acknowledgement and response to abuses of power and as Selina Stone says – reimagining a different future.

Professor Lisa Oakley
Chester University, April 2025

Introduction

My heart sinks and I let out a heavy sigh. Another story, another leader, another person or group of people harmed. It has become too common now – because abuses of power permeate so many aspects of our life together within the Church and also beyond. At a time when so many have lost faith in institutions including religious ones – and not just millennials and younger generations – each story confirms our suspicion is well founded. But underneath what can be perceived as cynicism are hurt, anger and frustration at the onslaught of abuses of power. And this disappointment is a sign that deep down many of us believe that things do not have to be this way – that abuses of power are not in fact inevitable. And this hope, this faith, is what drives us to figure out how to identify power and its uses and abuses, and how to safeguard ourselves and others against being the abuser or the abused.

So why does this keep on happening? The explanations come from far and wide. There has been a plethora of books written on the topic of unhealthy leadership or abuse in the last few years in particular. Many of them are written by church leaders, some of whom have experienced abuse in the religious contexts where they had responsibility for supporting others. And so we are reminded from the outset that the lines of power are not always straightforward. Many of these books come out of or focus on the US Evangelical world in particular, as the veil has been increasingly pulled back on patterns of abuse. We also have a few British interventions. Chuck DeGroat looks at the 'narcissism' of particular individuals who use their church as a platform for their self-actualization, trampling others in the process.[1] Others also examine the individual pastor or leader as failing to live up to Christian leadership ideals, most notably that of 'servant leadership'.[2] In other cases, we are invited to consider the tactics abusers use, particularly in religious contexts.[3] But to prevent us from making this about the failure of individuals, others have asked us to think about deeper cultural questions. Katelyn Beaty makes a compelling argument for concentrating on the cultures that enable abusive leaders, in particular our collective buying into the thrill of celebrity.[4] Laura Barringer and Scot McKnight invite us to consider how to create healthy churches that resist abusive patterns and leaders.[5] This approach is also taken by Justin Lewis Anthony in his account of Christian abuses of power, in which he questions the very notion of 'Christian leadership', labelling it a heresy.[6]

In reviewing this literature written for Christians and especially Christian leaders, rather than for academics, there is a distinct lack of a sustained attempt to examine a core thread in Christian abuse: Christian theology itself. The one example I could find was by Nicholas Peter Harvey and Linda Woodhead, who offer theological reflections in light of spiritual abuse in the Anglican and Roman Catholic traditions in their 2022 book *Unknowing God: Toward a Post-Abusive Theology*.[7] And one of the most important books on power and abuse, written by psychologist and counsellor Diane Langberg, *Redeeming Power* spends considerable time naming some of the theological problems in the wide-ranging contexts she has worked in.[8] Generally speaking, books that seek to deal with power and abuse, especially in Charismatic and Evangelical settings, hint at theology as a key factor in abuse but there is yet to be an in-depth account of what this looks like and what it means. This is not a criticism of the writers I have pointed to – no book can do everything and we are not all theologians, driven to focus on theology as I am. But this is an essential component of addressing abuses of power adequately. This is made clear in the work of Lisa Oakley and her colleagues, who have worked tirelessly to name and educate us on abuses of power in churches, which are often called 'spiritual abuse'.[9]

Power and theology

Whether in our interpersonal experiences, or the big events happening on a global stage, the power of theology and also our particular theologies of power are evident. All theologies have power, shaping our imagination in terms of how we see God, and ourselves. Theologies form a lens through which we interpret what we experience, and decide what we should do or not do. They inform our opinions when we watch the news and shape our attitudes to those we see as different. Often this happens on a subconscious level. But when I talk about theologies of power, I mean there are some theologies or theological emphases that have a particularly significant impact on how we recognize and respond to power. Certain theologies that we think might be totally benign and innocent can have huge ethical consequences – shaping our vision of a good life and how we live. There are certain theological ideas that, in my view, leave the door open (or even roll out a red carpet) for domination, abuse, bullying, violence – even death. They both enable those who behave in such ways by providing them with a narrative to support their behaviour, and convince the rest of us to accept it. Theologies can also, in contrast, provide safeguards, enabling us to promote righteousness (or justice), protect the vulnerable, and help to free those who are oppressed. This is a book about exposing the former and ensuring we cultivate the latter.

When we peel back the layers of our disagreements and debates, whether in churches, community groups, online or in the news, power is often lurking beneath the surface, even if not explicitly expressed. There are concerns about who has power – the answer is often 'the elite' or 'the privileged'. We have, in recent years, become better able to name the kinds of power we or others may inherit socially due to race, gender, class or other social constructs (ways we collectively categorize and assign meaning to different bodies). We might be able to recognize the disempowerment that impacts people living with disabilities or those who belong to sexual and gender minorities. Yet at the same time, those who feel threatened by historically ignored voices now feel themselves to be disempowered and under threat. The mainstream now claims to be the marginalized, and seeks to maintain its dominance in a clever sleight of hand. 'The oppressed' are now not only those who are tangibly impacted by forms of injustice and exclusion but whoever *feels* victimized or is made uncomfortable by hearing about the life experiences of the former group. It is increasingly the case that those who are used to saying and doing whatever they like now regard themselves as 'oppressed' whenever they are held to account.

The panic about power that shapes our cultural conversations is exacerbated for Christians whose faith has been dominated by Western cultural and philosophical norms. There is a desire to know what kinds of uses of power can be considered morally good – Christians will all cry that 'the power of God' is good but never quite explain what this means and how we know what God's power is like, and more importantly, is *not* like. Christians in Europe, and in the UK specifically, where I am writing, have enjoyed a history of establishment alongside the state, with all the benefits and blindness that come with it. European Christianity has known the 'success' of global expansion through colonialism and various forms of missionary activity, giving it a sense of divine favour. The decline in membership of Christian churches in Europe demands Christians come to terms with the loss of certain forms of power and privilege. This is even more true in contexts where people of many different faiths now live and hope to practise their faith. How do these postcolonial times force European churches to reimagine ecclesial power as empires die and evolve?

INTRODUCTION

The complexity of aligning with political power for spiritual objectives has led European churches to the kind of compromises that are only possible when the end and the means of Christian mission and ministry are separated. In more recent times, we have had to face the unravelling of a common dream that somehow contemporary Christians by virtue of our espoused faith could be trusted to resist the abuses of power seen in 'the world'. I use quotation marks, because the determination to draw a hard line between 'the Church' and 'the world' has consistently prevented us as Christians from reflecting on our own shameful behaviour. If 'the world' is godless and evil, and the Church is godly and good, then we are encouraged to judge the world in the harshest terms while extending excessive grace to the sins of 'the godly'. Christians then imagine that there is no need to be trained to understand sexual harassment, toxic behaviour and racist abuse, since these are 'worldly concerns'; instead, apparently, we simply need more Bible studies.

In recent years, various well-known and recognizably powerful pastors and leaders have been revealed as abusers of power. The revelations are appalling by any standards, let alone the ethics of Christ and the kin-dom[10] he came to embody and invite us into. The Church is called to be distinct in its obedience to God and the leading of the Spirit, and yet the love of power so often dominates this calling and the work of God in us. It seems unhelpful to act as if we are already what we hope to be. So let's lay down all our claims of distinctiveness, our desire to have people look at us and to us – and acknowledge that for the most part, there is no difference between what we see in terms of power, justice and ethics among Christians and in the 'world'. Rates of fair pay between genders, inclusive leadership, generosity and kindness, peace and fairness, respect of human dignity and human agency are not automatically better among Christians, and in fact can be decidedly worse. At times, understandings of the Bible and its implications for our lives together are at the core of this sad reality.

Christian theology is not straightforward when it comes to power, and though we might look with embarrassment at the behaviour of Christians in earlier times and others in the present, it is to some extent understandable that they landed at the conclusions we now lambast. The Hebrew Bible (that is, Old Testament) narratives present an elite group of people who have a special divine place in the plan and mind of God, and on this basis are commanded to massacre other people, take their land and own it for themselves. We find stories of a God who commands women to marry their rapists, sends a slave girl back to her oppressors, and does not use his power to free his own people when they are enslaved for 400 years. This is uncomfortable reading, but we must recognize that it is there and not ignore or overlook it if we are going to engage with the Bible with integrity.

Many of us will read such sections of the biblical text and be clear that this should not set ethical standards for how we live in contemporary contexts. We do not read divine commands to wipe people out and assume this gives us permission for genocide today. But we may still find ways to justify or at least allow some kinds of violence on the assumption that it might be permissible in God's eyes. While it may seem that asking WWJD (What Would Jesus Do?) gets us out of the predicament – since Jesus is sometimes regarded as the nicer person of the Trinity when compared to God the Father as seen in the Old Testament – the damage, for some, has already been done. With this background in place of a vengeful, violent God, Jesus is read as a fire-breathing gladiator figure who died, beat up the devil and came back from the dead. His Second Coming will be full of wrath, judgement and violence, and this is what some may (even secretly) long for, as a final 'gotcha'.

But in the biblical accounts, we find Jesus, God in flesh, born to a peasant family, carried in the body of a young woman without much to her name and laid in a trough where animals ate. Time and again we see that he was not welcomed by the people with power but by those who wandered on the edges of community. He could command crowds through his storytelling in which he painted a beautiful vision of life with God. And his actions of healing allowed people to experience that vision in their real lives. He was an influencer of sorts. But then he was crucified when these same crowds turned against him because he did not give them what they wanted. And, unconcerned about his personal legacy or his well-being, he was willing for this to happen because he discerned somehow that it was the will of God. We are left with a confusing vision of divine power. On the one hand, we have an all-powerful, commanding God who can control all things, which is interpreted by some as teaching us to build and hold on to almightiness. And on the other, we are taught, it seems, to let people harm us, to have few boundaries, to lay our lives down as a sacrifice even when evil people are the ones demanding it from us.

Why this book?

This book has been written to explore the theologies that in my view are implicated in the crises of power and abuse by leaders formed and functioning in Evangelical and Charismatic Christian communities. It was born in part because, after teaching a course on 'theologies of power' for an MA in Christian Leadership, my final cohort of students demanded I write a book on it. While my students included predominantly trainee priests in the Church of England (although I had a Church of England bishop in this class once!), I also welcomed Christian leaders from other denominations, youth ministers, consultants in the church- and faith-based charity sector, senior leaders of charities, experts in international development and those working in politics and business; anyone who wanted to examine what it meant to lead as a Christian in ways that avoided the pitfalls which have become apparent time and time again. The bulk of the sessions was given over to critical discussion in which the perspectives, experiences and critical engagement of the students took centre stage. I acted as a guide and a teacher, pointing them in the direction of deeper exploration as they examined their theological assumptions, the theory and practice of their own leadership and what they might learn from God and their peers. Though my writing was inspired by some of my own thoughts and questions through teaching this course, this book is entirely new and has been written from scratch, drawing on new research and exploring more urgent questions. Unlike my students, readers of this book will not face an essay question at the end, but of course that should not prevent you from writing and reflecting on the themes if you wish.

I have written this as a theologian who is deeply concerned with how Christian faith – both the beliefs we profess and the spiritual habits we develop – shape how we live and live with others. I do not assume that theology has the full antidote to the problem of abuses of power. But I do believe it is too often a major factor given minor attention. It is telling that what so many abusers of power in the Christian world have in common is regularly reading the Bible, prayer, commitment to ministry and mission, and holding to a particular notion of orthodoxy – and yet here we are. In writing this book I am addressing part of the conversation that as yet has not been dealt with in any comprehensive way. There is a battle for theological imagination that we must engage with as part of the attempts to address abuse in churches. And I hope this book will contribute to that work.

I also write as a theological educator who is very committed to allowing people to recognize their own theologies as theology even if they do not have formal qualifications. This is the theology I first learnt from my grandparents, parents and church family who gave me a foundation no university-validated course could. I also seek to ensure my own theological work is accessible and inviting for everyone who is interested. It is my view that Christian theology can never be confined to books and lecture halls – even if we sometimes try to keep it there. It is a living, growing, wild thing. It does not need to

INTRODUCTION

be written in a way that is overly academic – with so many footnotes it is off-putting, or with unnecessarily long words. This is often how we determine what counts as 'rigour' in the academic world, but it can do more harm than good for a book like this, written to be read by anyone, not just academics. It is baffling to me that we celebrate the kind of theological work that cannot be understood by those who desire to know God better. I consider it a personal failure as a theologian if I communicate in that way, even if that kind of writing is what gets you a promotion. And so this is a theological book on power and what we often call 'leadership' (a contested term I will discuss later) without hundreds of footnotes, but with as much deep thought and consideration as one that has them.

And finally, I write as a person who was raised in church, and has had numerous roles in the churches I have belonged to over the years. I have loved and been loved in the context of churches, and also experienced heartbreak and betrayal. I have felt the impact of Christian bullies in the workplace, and also in churches where egos rule the day. I have also glimpsed the beauty that is possible when we gather together out of a shared love for each other and for God. In more recent years I have served churches across denominations in various ways, without pinning myself to any particular tradition or congregation – despite some attempts. I am a trained community organizer who was taught how to analyse and understand how power actually works among people and organizations. I have researched leadership and well-being in church spaces, and come to understand the way race, gender and class also shape these experiences. I inhabit the world as a Black woman, raised in the inner city, with the privilege of viewing our institutions, including Christian ones, from a vantage point that allows me to see what others miss. I live through the wisdom of Black women, and all those who have always had to recognize and tap into their own power while it has been denied and trampled by others. I write as one who has been taught by the women of my natural and spiritual family to discern the powers – seen and unseen – and to do battle with them simply to survive. I depend on womanists and other theological ethicists who, like other feminists, help us recognize that we cannot really understand power and abuse without attending to how the dynamics of gender, as well as race and class and other aspects of our identity, inform our relationships. All of this influences the themes and stories I have chosen to explore. I write for the weary, the overworked, those denied ordination unjustly, the exhausted, unpaid and underpaid workers. I write for those who may consider themselves 'deconstructing' or 'decolonising', or at least asking what it is all for. It is an attempt to contribute to the 'theological remaking' that Karen O'Donnell teaches us is necessary for those of us who have survived or are surviving kinds of trauma.[11] I hold in my mind and heart those exploited, financially, sexually or emotionally, by people who should have cared for them. I think of those sworn to secrecy, those threatened into silence, and those who knew to be quiet about what happened even without being told. We are the survivors, the bruised, the living, who testify.

Throughout the book you will read reflections on particular cases, with individuals named. Please tread especially carefully if you have been personally affected by stories of abuse that have hit the headlines. We can only imagine how many other cases of abuse there are, in congregations and contexts where the spotlight has not fallen because the leader is not well known or the congregation is not particularly large. I have not chosen these cases because they are more important, but because there has been enough investigation, from a good enough range of places, that has been made public. This enables us to look at them, to learn lessons that may help us in the lesser-known cases that may mirror at least some of what has taken place. These cases may seem extreme and therefore the risk is that some may feel that since they would never be like [fill in the blank] they do not need to worry. To them I would say that these cases, for me, represent the wide edge of the wedge, or somewhere down a slippery slope, at the top of which all of us with some power over others sit. To put it in scriptural terms, these cases exemplify 'full-grown' sin, that begins as a desire that is conceived from a seed, and eventually gives birth to death (James 1.15).

There may be concern among some readers about whether we really do have an obligation to rethink theology due to ethical concerns. Are we at risk of throwing the baby out with the bath water? The discernment between good and bad theology is, in my view, in part determined by the fruit it produces. If a particular doctrinal position or emphasis in our theology nurtures goodness or what we might call 'godliness', then I think we have got quite close to an accurate view of things. Is this particular theological position enabling me, or us, to love God more faithfully – which in Jesus' own words is intrinsically linked to loving ourselves and our neighbour? Or does it move us further away or cause us to be imbalanced by loving ourselves over loving God and neighbour, or loving our neighbour in a way that harms ourselves and dishonours God who has made us? It is not a simple thing to discern what to do when our theologies cause us problems, but I do think we have a responsibility to rethink and revisit what we have set in our minds as 'true' when we start to notice it is having harmful effects. This is, in part, what I gather from Jesus' 'You've heard it said ... but I say' statements in Matthew 5. The chapter begins with Jesus saying he has not come to abolish the law, but to fulfil it, and then he encourages them to critically engage with the traditions they have inherited. There is an invitation here to recognize that theology and the ethics we derive from it are not static, but must be continually discerned as our circumstances, experiences and contexts change.

Ultimately, I write this book because I believe something else is possible, and I have been fortunate enough to experience it. I have worked in an organization where my vocation mattered, not just what I produced. This has stayed with me even when I worked in places where this has not been the case. I know what it is to experience the kind of pastoral care that is sensitive and insightful and appropriately boundaried. I have experienced being led by someone both brilliant and kind, who was not particularly charismatic, but had many spiritual gifts in serving God and others. I know other realities are possible and I want to see them become more prominent in our collective experience and consciousness than the bad cases that seem to dominate.

Structure

This book comprises seven chapters, each dealing with a particular theme and theological problem which relates to power.

Chapter 1 explores how we should understand power, as breath given by God, and then as the dynamics of relationships and interests. Power, in theological terms, begins with God, and then becomes something we construct and define through our interpersonal and social connections. I then consider how to define abuses of power in Christian contexts.

Chapter 2 provides an examination of the power of words, with a focus on the Charismatic traditions that have been highlighted in notable cases of spiritual abuse in recent years. I explore ideas of 'calling' and 'gifting' and how they convey power to individuals, sometimes unduly. I think about preaching as a particular exercise of power, and how preaching can be used to groom congregations to accept abuse.

In Chapter 3, I examine how theologies that present a particular notion of 'the work of God' as almighty and dominant can support abusive dynamics. Here, I think through the capitalistic notions of success and numerical growth that can trip us up when it comes to recognizing and exposing abuse of power in the Church. These expansionist narratives are contrasted with parables of the kingdom that value the small things, and a gospel that champions 'the weak'.

Chapter 4 discusses principalities and powers, not as a 'secular' aspect of our reality, but as a dimension of church life and Christian institutions. Challenging the binary that promotes hyper-vigilance regarding 'the world' and a lack of wise boundaries and discernment in the context of 'the Church', I look at the parable of the wheat and tares as a way forward.

In Chapter 5 we deal with one of the most significant theological power questions, that of theologies of suffering and sacrifice, and the abuse they can engender. Here I bring womanist (Black feminist) theology – which has (along with feminism across the board) long critiqued the way atonement theories can sacralize violence – to bear on the case of John Smyth, who shed the blood of his victims through beatings.

In Chapter 6 I explore the theme of vulnerability, which has become more complicated in recent years. Thinking through the way vulnerability is lauded by writers like Brené Brown, I consider the way humility (a vulnerable posture) can be utilized to further empower the powerful. In particular I examine the way the 'servant leader' motif can undermine attentiveness to power. I also focus on the complexity of using Jesus as a model for good leadership, and especially in his embrace of vulnerability.

In the final chapter, I ask what we might do, in light of the reality that we cannot uncover all of the wolves among us, or even the wolf who might be within us. Here I discuss discernment as crucial to safeguarding ourselves and others in the community of faith. I explore discernment as a spiritual gift given by God, but also a skill cultivated through paying attention to embodied knowledge, and the stories we would rather not hear.

Notes

1 Chuck DeGroat, *When Narcissism Comes to Church: Healing Your Community from Emotional and Spiritual Abuse* (Downer's Grove, IL: IVP, 2020).

2 Marcus Honeysett, *Powerful Leaders: When Church Leadership Goes Wrong and How to Prevent It* (London: IVP, 2022); Jamin Goggin and Kyle Strobel, *The Way of the Dragon or the Way of the*

Lamb: Searching for Jesus' Path of Power in a Church that Has Abandoned It (Nashville, TN: Nelson Books, 2017); Andy Crouch, *Playing God – Redeeming the Gift of Power* (Downer's Grove, IL: IVP, 2013).

3 Wade Mullen, *Something's Not Right: Decoding the Hidden Tactics of Abuse and Freeing Yourself from Its Power* (Carol Stream, IL: Tyndale Momentum, 2020); Michael J. Kruger, *Bully Pulpit: Confronting the Problem of Spiritual Abuse in the Church* (Grand Rapids, MI: Zondervan, 2022).

4 Katelyn Beaty, *Celebrities for Jesus: How Personas, Platforms and Profits are Hurting the Church* (Grand Rapids, MI: Brazos Press, 2022).

5 Laura Barringer and Scot McKnight, *A Church Called Tov: Forming a Goodness Culture that Resists Abuses of Power and Promotes Healing* (Carol Stream, IL: Tyndale House Publishers, 2020).

6 Justin Lewis-Anthony, *You are the Messiah and I Should Know: Why Leadership is a Myth (and Probably a Heresy)* (London: Bloomsbury, 2013).

7 Nicholas Peter Harvey and Linda Woodhead, *Unknowing God: Toward a Post-Abusive Theology* (Eugene, OR: Cascade Books, 2022).

8 Diane Langberg, *Redeeming Power: Understanding Authority and Abuse in the Church* (Grand Rapids, MI: Brazos Press, 2020).

9 Lisa Oakley and Justin Humphreys, *Escaping the Maze of Spiritual Abuse: Creating Healthy Christian Cultures* (London: SPCK, 2019).

10 I am keen to adopt the meaning of 'kin-dom' to convey family ties born of the reign of God, rather than the kind of dominance and control that 'kingdom' can convey. So even when I say kingdom, in keeping with the language of the text, please do hear kin-dom. I first discovered the use of this term in the work of mujerista (Latin American feminist) theologian Ada María Isasi-Díaz, who credits Georgene Wilson OSF with teaching it to her. For these women, kin-dom is a more accurate labelling of what Jesus came to establish: familial bonds of love, justice and mercy rather than the hierarchies of patriarchal domination implied by 'kingdom'. It is also more reflective of the centrality of family in the lives of Latinas. See Ada María Isasi-Díaz, *Mujerista Theology: A Theology for the Twenty-First Century* (Maryknoll, NY: Orbis Books, 1996), p. 83, n14.

11 Karen O'Donnell, *Survival: Radical Spiritual Practices for Trauma Survivors* (London: SCM Press, 2024), p. 22.

I

Power and Theology

> When powerful people say they have no power, they really mean they don't have as much power as they'd like. (Father Simon Cuff)

The quotation above was the reply of a friend after I ranted to him about a recent encounter I had had with a very powerful figure in the UK church. I exclaimed that I had never in my life met so many people who had so much power and yet repeatedly claimed to have none. These individuals had people's jobs, housing, families and well-being in their hands. With one decision they could bring about a person's dream or nightmare, and their choices affected hundreds if not thousands of people. Yet I had met such a person who, when asked a very specific question about his lack of action, rubbed his head and declared, 'People think I have power, but I have none.' Immediately the dynamic in the meeting shifted from attempting to hold him accountable, to consoling him and responding to his performance of being overwhelmed. I even felt my own posture change – maybe I had been too harsh in my expectations? Surely he was telling the truth about what he could and could not do? The meeting moved on. He no longer had to explain himself.

Power is a complex thing to pin down, but that is exactly what I am going to try to do in this first chapter. It is important to begin by explaining what I do and do not mean by such a broad word, the definition of which has been much discussed. The focus of this book is on how power works in and through theology. I am concerned with some of the ideas about power we find in Christian theology, and how theology becomes a tool through which power – and in particular the abuse of power – functions. This is, for me, a question that centres on the Bible, the ideas and traditions Christians have drawn from it over centuries, the life of the Christian community both now and in history, and the experiences of individuals within these communities. But power, as it appears in and through theology, the Bible and lived experience, is complex. It functions on many different levels in our lives and communities and can bring many images and ideas to mind. These ideas have been formed by a whole range of people, with a range of expertise. Some are philosophers or theologians whose writings have seeped into our collective imagination for so long that we do not recognize them. Some are activists, journalists, researchers, counsellors or psychotherapists who daily come face to face with the impact power has on people, for good or for ill. Some are social scientists, political theorists or cultural analysts who seek to name who has power and who does not, and what it means for life now and in the future. I will engage with a wide range of voices in this book, because understanding power depends on crossing disciplinary boundaries. I am the kind of theologian who is willing to recognize the limits of theology and the Bible for naming how things actually work in the world, including in relation to power. In order to understand power, we need to embrace the wisdom of people beyond the Church, the discipline of theology and biblical texts. There is much for us to recognize and understand.

Those of us who value theology or work as theologians might be tempted to talk about power in very idealistic ways. When we start with the Bible, we are quick to paint an idealized picture of power, where we focus on helping people to see what we are aiming for. We might speak repeatedly about 'servant leadership' as an ideal and an objective, but this does not help much if we don't tell the truth about the other theological ideas circulating which send us in the opposite direction. There is much complexity in the discussion of leadership, power, God and the Church, and we need to think through the complex nuances both of what they might mean theoretically and of what they might actually look like in practice. We must diagnose the illness properly before attempting to write a prescription. The diagnostic work requires many voices and perspectives and we tend to need more than what usually falls within the realm of theology. I will throughout this chapter and the book hold together the theological with what we might call the ethical or practical – even political. The beliefs we hold about God will be considered alongside questions about what constitutes the right way to be or act as Christians.

This chapter commences with a straightforwardly theological account of power that starts with God. I do not begin my definition of power by thinking about relationships between people – what we might think of as power in its social or political forms. These definitions, devised by philosophers or sociologists (and sometimes theologians!), matter a lot, but by starting with God, the source of all that is, we might be properly oriented to the theme and issues at hand. When we begin with thinking of power as something we human beings define, possess, or create, we end up giving undue authority to the uses and abuses of power that we have chosen or experienced and are more familiar to us. This is one of the problems with power and abuse – that we too often assume that power is ours to have, use and define as we see fit and for our own ends. Beginning with definitions rooted in human action – even when they are good and helpful to resist abuse – falls into this same trap. I begin instead with a reminder that the power of the divine breath is the origin of all things, and what allows all that exists to exist. Without the divine breath being given to us for our own breathing, there would be no relationships in which we experience power, no institutions through which to hold and exert power, no campaigns through which we might build and exert power. God as the garden in which all exist and grow, the womb in which we 'live and move and have our being' (Acts 17.28), is the beginning of power.

Following the pattern of creation which then brings relationships between human beings into existence, I then discuss the social dynamics of power that shape our experiences of community. This will include the matters of belonging among us on an interpersonal level, as well as the way power functions in favour of and against groups in our social structures. I then focus squarely on theology and abuse in UK churches, with the help of Lisa Oakley and Justin Humphreys in their book *Escaping the Maze of Spiritual Abuse*, which helps us to think deeply about abuse, power and healthy communities in the British context.

Power as breath: A theological foundation

I write with an understanding that we all have power. By this, I do not mean that we can all have the life we want if we believe it or just put our minds to it. Nor do I mean that we all have a voice that others hear, the capacity to 'make things happen' as we want or access to the resources and influence we desire. I do not mean it in the ways I learnt as a community organizer where we spoke about all of us having power, defined as the 'ability to act'. This is the common definition: power is the way we get things done. This makes sense for many of us, but at the same time, it is not true for all kinds of people. Those living under oppressive authoritarian governments might have little to no power to enact their will individually or collectively. People who are gravely ill in mind or body may not have the capacity to exert agency in relation to their own lives, let alone have any kind of power in relationship with others. Those held in captivity, or enslaved, or living under violent dictators or the threat of militias may hold on to a sense of inner power in terms of their belief in their dignity and self-worth despite how they are treated. They might even find relatively small ways to subvert their domination, but overall, can they be said to have power if power is about action, having a say, or choosing the path one desires? No.

These functional definitions of power and powerlessness are very important when we are thinking about the social and political dynamics of power. It is important that we can identify who has power and who does not if we are at all concerned about human flourishing, justice and equality for all made in God's image. But, for me, thinking about power theologically must begin with a focus on divine power, and especially divine power at the beginning of all things.

Diane Langberg, an expert in spiritual abuse in Christian communities, begins her theology of power in Genesis 1, with the verse, 'Let Us make man in Our image, according to Our likeness; and let them rule over the fish of the sea and over the birds of the sky and over the cattle and over all the earth, and over every creeping thing that creeps on the earth.'[1] This starting point, for Langberg, makes it clear that power is divinely given; there are no abusive hierarchies of domination and exploitation, simply shared responsibility to care for God's creation. In her words, 'God gave humans power in that they might bear God's character in the world.'[2] They are given power in order to do good, and to be divine representatives. This is, for Langberg, an important corrective to ideas about power which suggest that God has designed us to live in patterns of control and domination over each other. It reminds us all that power does not begin with us. But as I have already said, this functional definition of power is far from the real capacity of many people for different reasons.

Functional definitions of power, even when rooted in Scripture, do not provide a firm enough foundation for how we might define power theologically, because they cannot be said to be true of all people. There is a problem, in my view, if our baseline definition of power is ableist because it only applies to those with a particular set of physical or mental capacities. This is the impression I get from the Genesis command: we are given an image of the first humans roaming around stewarding creation. How does this relate to people who for whatever reason could not have walked around to interact with animals or may not have even been able to see or remember them? Are these individuals now 'powerless', or failing to fulfil their divine purpose as human beings to exert power? A theological definition of power is inadequate if it so clearly betrays human biases. If our theological definition of power is solely or predominantly accessible to those with particular bodies or backgrounds, while excluding others, we should be mindful of the likelihood that we are projecting our own human failings onto God. When in churches we can find that because of their race, gender, sexuality, class, and/or being neurotypical or considered able-bodied, certain people are more trusted than others to 'bear God's character in the world',[3] we might believe that God prefers that kind of human to represent God. We might begin to suspect that there is a hierarchy within our human family as to who really should have power to 'rule over' and who should be ruled. Power, when defined theologically, must begin in and with God, and be justly applicable to all humanity as those made in the image of God. No individual or group can be abandoned, left behind or considered to 'not fit' when we define what power is and how God has made it available to us as human beings.

At the most basic level, a theology of power must be said to be true for all people regardless of age, sex, socio-economic status, living situation, sexuality, ethnicity or race, state of health or well-being. Otherwise, we end up with a theology that favours some – such as those who are able-bodied or living in democratic societies – over others. And by extension, it then seems that God has favourites, those whom God has been careful to care for, and on whom God has been careful to bestow power, and others whom God has neglected or who fail to live up to this ideal. When I say we all have power, I am thinking of the most basic level of what it means to be human and alive. I am imagining the moment in which God breathes *'ruach'* (spirit) into humanity in Genesis 1 and God's life becomes our life. This is for me the start of what it means for us to have power. Power is first and foremost breath. It is the moment that humanity goes from being a pile of reddish-brown-black soil formed into a human shape, into a living being with a name. Power in a theological sense is God's life and being, gifting life and being to us and all creation. Power is, in the words of James Poling, 'virtually synonymous with life itself'[4] when in its ideal (partly what I mean by divine) form. To have power is to be, to breathe, to live. But this divine power goes beyond us as human beings. Few of us would doubt the power of the waves of the sea, or the wind howling in a hurricane. Power is breath, life and existence. It comes to us in the act of creation by God, the eternal life source, who gives rise to all possibilities. And even when as individuals we have given up our last breath, however we come to that moment, we continue to be held within the breath of God and experience ongoing power in the life to come. This power is not limited to our material existence; it cannot ultimately be taken from us.

This theological basis of power is often overlooked in the conversations we have about power, which focus on the social and political. But it is important to start here, in order for us to recognize the dignity and value of every human person, regardless of the distortions of power we see in our social, political and economic life locally, nationally and globally. The primacy of breath as power is born out of the reality that, regardless of the racial, socio-economic and gendered oppressions that sought to disempower my ancestors, they lived and retained a kind of power. They were not powerless. Despite the systemic and structural threats of figurative, if not literal, suffocation, many individuals and groups have lived with a kind of power that allowed them to strive for, build and create life for themselves and others. It is the kind of power described by feminist theologian Rita Nakashima Brock, when she says:

> The fundamental power of life, born into us, heals, makes whole, empowers, and liberates. Its manifold forms create and emerge from heart, that graceful, passionate mystery

at the center of ourselves and each other. This power heals brokenheartedness and gives courage to the fainthearted.[5]

When we forget to think of power as beginning with divine breath to all, or when we betray this theological understanding, the consequences are dire, and manifest in social and political power inequalities. It can mean that we collectively hope for breath to be extended to members of the royal family when diagnosed with a critical illness, while failing to hold sacred the breath of children in Gaza. It would be remiss of us to imagine that the life and being of the natural world should be an afterthought in such conversations, when it was called good by God before we were, and we cannot exist without it. It is not only in God that we live and move and have being, but in the world of oceans, trees and the atmosphere, which are being depleted at ever more alarming rates.

Power as breath, as divine breath, is power at the most fundamental level, which is what it is because of the generosity of God and the life of the Spirit. This power is given to us all by God; it is universal. After this, power gets much more complicated. This is because we do not only relate to God, whose power is given to us first as spirit, but we also exist in relationship with others. These relationships between us, as human beings, are marked by power. We see this clearly in the Genesis story. It is not long before this simple image of power, in which humanity depends on the loving creative presence of God, is distorted. The serpent uses the power of its breath and the power of knowledge to deceive the first humans and introduce shame into their experience. The perceived competition between Cain and Abel leads Cain to use his power to end his brother's life. What we learn from this is that in our social relationships, it is easy to lose sight of the inherent, divinely given power of life and breath. When we forget this, our use of power can easily become misdirected.

Power in relationships

I once heard it said that when men speak about power, they mean power over others, and when women speak about power, we simply mean power over ourselves. I am sure this is not true across the board, but it rang true to me because I see this tension between different meanings of power in the debates that shape much of our contemporary life. For those of us who belong to groups that have been historically told by others what we can and cannot be, do or have, we are often simply fighting for the agency to make choices for ourselves. Yet we live in a world where others, who get to decide for themselves, refuse us the same power. Those who will not be impacted at all by the issue at hand, in terms of their own freedoms and choices, seek to make themselves lords over us. It is important that we begin our thoughts on power in relationships with an awareness that too often what is happening is not a tension between two powers who simply disagree, and should do so 'well'.[6] What is at stake is one group who simply want to exist and have a good life, and others who for whatever reason want to use their power to deny this possibility in one way or another. This is, by definition, an abuse of power, a refusal to allow people to have a say over their own lives, and instead to dominate them by imposing someone else's will on to them. This imposed will is often cited as God's but is in reality simply an interpretation of God's will.

In the reality of our social relationships – both on an interpersonal level and in a broader structural sense – there are multiple forms and dynamics of power that cause us to dishonour the divine breath gifted to each of us, no matter the body we inhabit. These dynamics are created, and often sustained, by us collectively, though sometimes unknowingly. They are not inevitable as God's divine breath is, but they are constructed by us and stubborn. They are the result of human action or our refusal to act. Diane Langberg lists the types of human power she has encountered in her work on abuse in churches, including: verbal power and silence, physical size and strength, personality, specialized knowledge, positions of authority, absence (neglect), economic or financial power, spiritual power and cultural power.[7] This list represents the kinds of power people can possess (for example, over money or decisions), as well as the elements of their identity that can make it easier for someone to attain power (such as their personality). In addition to this, Oakley and Humphreys explain that power can function in 'bottom up' ways, as well as 'top down', in faith communities.[8] By this they mean that it is not only the leaders in positions of power who are at risk of abusing it, but those in congregations who hold sway over the individuals who serve them in various ways. Power can be linked to the capacity to coerce and control through numbers.

In understanding dynamics of power in our churches, we might also add the ways different aspects of our identity can result in power, or disempowerment, in ways we can fail to notice. There is a ton of academic literature as well as more publicly accessible books written on these themes of late, by those within Christian spaces and beyond. They help us attend to these issues, even if they do not use 'power' language explicitly. Race is a social construct which conveys huge power in many settings if you are considered white, and disempowers those of us who are not. Gender, another construct, linked to sex (the biological distinctions we have), has been used to limit women's power in the home, churches and wider society. There is a kind of social power that comes with being in a heterosexual marriage in Christian contexts, which evades those who are unmarried. This can feel even more true for women, as our value and trustworthiness are so often tied to the status of 'wife' and 'mother'. Class divisions reflect financial, social and economic power, or the lack thereof, and can shape whether or not you are trusted with positions of authority in some settings. Views on human sexuality and gender mean those who identify as LGBTQIA+ are targeted by forms of violent power in countries around the world, whether through threats of imprisonment, discrimination or even death. Disability activists have brought to the fore the ways people with disabilities are disempowered through the assumptions others make, and the refusal to make adequate adjustments. These aspects of power cannot be overlooked as we think about what contributes to the dynamics of social power at work in our contexts.

Power is attached to many elements of our lives and identities. The 'ability to act' is not universal; it is tied to particular socio-economic realities which determine what you can do and how you spend your time. Social relationships (who you know or do *not* know) have a huge impact on your ability to make things happen, and your cultural background so often impacts the relationships you can develop. It is for this reason that power cannot be discussed outside of facing the realities of identity, status, inequality or even oppression. We also feel very differently when some people use their power, as opposed to when others do. We should be familiar with the ways women are viewed and treated if we seek to 'act'. We can be labelled 'bossy' or domineering in contrast to men who, when acting in the same way, are just seen as assertive or confident.

Within these social dynamics of power, we find the particular realities of positional power and who is represented or absent. Whether in government, the Church, businesses or social organizations, power is often held by a small group of individuals who make decisions, set direction and manage processes and people. Ways of doing this vary widely, and this explains in part why leadership books and podcasts have become so popular in recent years, including for Christians. Church leaders have sought to draw on the patterns of those with power outside the Church who are believed to model success (understood as numerical growth). And this has involved attempts to merge this with Christian theology, to develop 'Christian leadership', most commonly through a particular reading of Jesus as presenting a countercultural model of leadership as a 'servant leader'. This has become the key phrase to describe how Christian leaders should understand the purpose of their power. Christians know that it is no longer cool to present as a dominating visionary who does not care for people. The language of 'servant leadership' is now bandied about, sometimes as nothing more than a kind of virtue signal that can distract people from asking, 'Is this what he is actually doing?'

Few of us want to admit that the phrase 'servant leader' is not the simplest thing to understand, let alone practise. It can even strike us as an oxymoron. A servant is led by someone else, and by that definition is not the leader, at least in relation to the one who is leading them. They may be a leader of other servants, while being a servant to the ultimate leader; this is the only way in which this works. This is often the way it is explained theologically. In the hierarchy of power (and power in our imagination is often about hierarchy) God is at the top, then the 'servant leader' is underneath, then the people they lead are at the bottom. But the 'servant leader' in the middle tends to be a man who claims to be modelling 'servant leadership' – and he might be honest in this desire – while having immense power and little accountability. He has the power to hire and fire at will; controls the money (whether formally or informally); is recognized as the visual representation of the organization; has ensured his friends surround him and requires little accountability. He may by virtue of his position have been able to establish strong relationships with leaders as powerful as himself, if not more so, to keep him safe if anything jeopardizes his position. He is all leader and not much of a servant in *practice* even if the *language* of servanthood is there. We will come back to this in detail later.

When we look at those who have been given positions of power and authority, it is easier to see the signs of our collective preferences for certain kinds of people to be trusted with power. We may not individually subscribe to the outcome, but as a group, whether in a church denomination, a local neighbourhood, a business or organization, or a nation, some form of collective is deciding who has power. This might be because they went to the right school or university, they speak with a certain accent (or lack of accent) or can present themselves according to particular cultural norms we define as 'professional'. They may have a particular kind of personality or demeanour, even a sense of humour that 'fits'. We have continued to see that those who have gone to the 'best universities' (when 'best' often just means the most exclusive) should not necessarily be trusted with power and leadership. But it seems that there is a persistent social hierarchy in which those in the upper classes, with more formal education, more money and without regional accents (Go, Brummies!), are trusted as more intelligent and worthy to hold power. We trust and give power to those who 'look like leaders' and speak with confidence (which is not at all a sign that they know what they are talking about) – we do not all benefit from such trust equally.

Though race and gender can be factors that prevent people ascending to certain heights, in other cases they are used as a tool to enable wider objectives. This is how I read the ascendency of various GMH (Global Majority Heritage) leaders within the Conservative party. The high-profile 'BAME' (Black, Asian and Minority Ethnic) figures could be claimed as a win for representation, while their politics take Britain further away from the interests of those they were presumed to represent. We should all be past the point of thinking having individuals from certain groups visually represented means that they will embrace the mission of ensuring diverse perspectives are heard. In our conversations about race and inclusion, there is an often unspoken power struggle taking place, between those who hope to retain the dominance of white (often English) cultural traditions and norms, and the diverse perspectives of those usually treated as 'other' who are seeking to be accepted as part of the mainstream. The divide between those who are for the status quo, and those who want to undo it, does not necessarily fall along racial lines.

But in this explanation of power, I am still speaking about positions, organizations, systems and structures, when the matter of personal relationships is often where we feel these power issues the most. In churches and Christian organizations the matter of power, vulnerability and leadership is deeply personal. It is naive of us to imagine that power dynamics do not have an impact on the relationships we have, whether we like them to or not. This is true of the pastor and their congregation, the team leaders and the team member, but also the more 'mature' believer and the new convert, the single woman in a world of married couples, the enthusiastic graduate and the impressive Christian organization working for a good cause. Some will say that I am cynical, that a church, charity or faith-based organization which professes a love of God and people is a place of family and friendship, where trust should take primary place over analyses of power. We might wish this to be true, but the language of 'family' very rarely matches the experience of being treated as a commodity or drained to support a vision you had no say in. We do not have to look too far to see how abuses of power thrive in places where there is hope and trust without any critical reflection on the dynamics of power shaping all these interactions. Stories abound in which leaders have led entire communities to ruin after exhibiting patterns of behaviour that should have rung alarm bells but did not. Why? Because, I want to argue, few (if any) people involved paid attention to how theology was enabling certain power dynamics that made spiritual abuse more likely, if not inevitable.

The power of theology and abuse in the Church

We are greatly indebted in the UK – whether or not we recognize it – to the work of Lisa Oakley, who has committed so much of her career to understanding and educating us about abuse in religious contexts, along with various collaborators. Along with Justin Humphreys, she has thankfully written a very accessible and affordable version of the research she conducted with Kathryn Kinmond, entitled *Escaping the Maze of Spiritual Abuse: Creating Healthy Christian Cultures*.[9] Though it is not a theological book, theology and the use of Scripture come up throughout the book as major factors in spiritual abuse. As I mentioned, this was one of the factors motivating my writing of this book, and so it is important to give a little background on what Oakley and her research point us towards.

First, though defining the most complex experiences is no easy feat, Oakley and Kinmond offer a definition of spiritual abuse which is born out of their extensive conversations and research. In judging whether something is abusive or not, Oakley and Kinmond encourage us to see behaviour on a spectrum with healthy behaviour on one end, and abusive behaviour on the other, with many shades in between. In other words, it is not always straightforward or a clear binary – there is a need for deep reflection and discernment. We must pay attention to both one-off incidents, and patterns. Both are abuse and can be traumatic for survivors, but often abusers display a pattern of behaviour, which helps us spot abuse more easily. Their research also tells us to resist thinking that only leaders are perpetrators; abuse can happen in a top-down or bottom-up manner. Congregations can also abuse their priests, leaders and communities. This was evident to me in the research I did on clergy well-being that revealed the racial abuse minority ethnic clergy can experience at the hands of those they seek to serve.[10] In this book I focus on leaders, since my interest is the role of theology, which tends to be mediated through ordained or lay leaders who have had theological training and are the main or sometimes the sole voice in the pulpit. The pulpit is itself a place of great power, often guarded by those abusing those in their care.[11] Oakley and Kinmond are clear that definitions are inevitably contextual and never static – meaning they change as we learn more – but this is a good starting point:

> Spiritual Abuse (SA) is coercion and control of one individual by another in a spiritual context. The target experiences SA as a deeply emotional personal attack. This abuse may include: manipulation and exploitation, enforced accountability, censorship of decision making, requirements for secrecy and silence, pressure to conform, misuse of scripture or the pulpit to control behaviour, requirement of obedience to the abuser, the suggestion that the abuser has a 'divine' position and isolation from others, especially those external to the abusive context.[12]

Theology is implicated explicitly in this definition, in the 'misuse of scripture' and the 'suggestion that the abuser has a "divine position"'. I do not take this to mean that it is inherently abusive to suggest that a person is called by God to be, say, a pastor or priest. Rather, in abusive contexts, this is emphasized to enable abuse by suggesting that person should not be held accountable in the ways others are. This is especially seen in the use of the person's 'calling' as justification for quelling accusations or survivor testimony. Aside from these more obvious examples, theology is, I want to suggest, also implicated in the other examples of how spiritual abuse can manifest. Theologies can be used to manipulate people financially, by causing them to give out of shame, out of fear of divine punishment or under false promises of material return. Theologies about holiness – that of the leader and the lack of it on the part of the congregant – can be used to push a culture of inappropriate accountability. The theological chipping away of people's sense of agency and their capacity to set boundaries, through constant talks about obedience and humility, can easily enable censorship, demands for secrecy and silence, and pressure to conform. Theologies that encourage an 'us' and 'them' approach to the wider church, or family and friends, encourage isolation.

Theology is written all over spiritual abuse and this is what I hope to explore, with particular reference to the Charismatic and Evangelical parts of the Church that I know best. We are fortunate that, in addition to some American attempts to discuss spiritual abuse and theology, Nicholas Peter Harvey and Linda Woodhead have helped us in the UK to reflect on theology and spiritual abuse in the Anglican and Roman Catholic traditions.[13] There have been hints at the need for reflection on what is going wrong in the churches that tend to be the largest and fastest-growing in recent history. Far from embracing the assumption that there are simply 'bad apples', we must, in my view, take a good hard look at the tree and the roots.

Notes

1 Genesis 1.28, quoted in Diane Langberg, *Redeeming Power: Understanding Authority and Abuse in the Church* (Grand Rapids, MI: Brazos Press, 2020), p. 5.

2 Langberg, *Redeeming Power*, p. 6.

3 Langberg, *Redeeming Power*, p. 6.

4 James N. Poling, *The Abuse of Power: A Theological Problem* (Nashville, TN: Abingdon Press, 1991), p. 24.

5 Rita Nakashima Brock, *Journeys by Heart: A Christology of Erotic Power* (New York: Crossroad, 1988), p. 25.

6 As a side note, I do think this concern with 'disagreeing well' sometimes comes across (even if this is not intended) as a deeply classist English cultural concern that suggests politeness is more important than telling the profound truth about the harm being done. When 'disagreeing well' is about how we talk to each other online, I do agree in part. But too often in my experience, it is pushed by the kind of privileged upper-middle-class white person (often male) who finds emotions awkward, does not want to encounter the (even righteous) anger of others, and has very little or nothing at stake in the debate.

7 Langberg, *Redeeming Power*, pp. 8–10.

8 Lisa Oakley and Justin Humphreys, *Escaping the Maze of Spiritual Abuse: Creating Healthy Christian Cultures* (London: SPCK, 2019), p. 9.

9 For the academic monograph, see Lisa Oakley and Kathryn Kinmond, *Breaking the Silence on Spiritual Abuse* (London: Palgrave Macmillan, 2013).

10 Selina Stone, *'If It Wasn't for God': A Report on the Wellbeing of Global Majority Heritage Clergy in the Church of England* (London: The Church of England, 2022).

11 Oakley and Kinmond, *Breaking the Silence*, p. 46.

12 Oakley and Kinmond, *Breaking the Silence*, p. 21.

13 Nicholas Peter Harvey and Linda Woodhead, *Unknowing God: Toward a Post-Abusive Theology* (Eugene, OR: Cascade Books, 2022).

2

Words from God?
Calling, Power and Speech

When we take a look at the many stories of Christian leaders who abuse their power, we might draw the conclusion that we are easily misled by charismatic figures who know how to pull a crowd. This is a common risk across Christian traditions and contexts. It is particularly common for these figures to be men, because our Christian spaces have been shaped by (and have upheld) patriarchal ideals for centuries. Theology plays an important role in elevating the figure of the charismatic male leader, in the minds of individuals and in the collective imagination of believers. When we listen back to the accounts of survivors and observers, we find certain theological ideas underpinning the willingness people have to let their guard down and allow these figures to influence their behaviour. One is the idea that the person is a 'man of God', whom God has chosen for a special purpose, that of allowing people to encounter God. Testimonies may abound about how a leader, who turns out to be abusive, created a movement through which many people came to faith and grew in faith. But underneath were patterns of abusive behaviour. The second idea is born from the first: that these individuals are believed to speak for God, to channel God's words to the congregation. There are many cases where spiritual gifts have been genuinely present and have been used to encourage and bless. However, great emphasis is put on the gifts of a particular individual, and an unhealthy level of dependency develops between this person and the congregation. People long to hear this person's voice, experienced as divine approval, despite issues with character and patterns of unhealthy behaviour. Oakley and Humphreys explain it this way in *Escaping the Maze of Spiritual Abuse*:

> In the experience of spiritual abuse sometimes people can be told that they cannot question or disagree with an individual or individuals because that person is God's anointed or chosen one ... sometimes there can be a suggestion that the abuser is the only person who can really hear from or speak to God and this puts them in a position of significant power ... So, while we would not dispute the notion of people being called and anointed, we would argue that this does not place people above question.[1]

As a result of these two ideas – that the person is called by God, and speaks for God – people defend the person who is abusing their power when accusations emerge. These two ideas act as a theological shield, as people start to believe (even subconsciously) that the abuse is a small price to pay for the wider good this person is believed to be doing. Even if they don't go as far as defending the abuser, people can be reluctant to report abuse, or want to silence victims, because they fear that holding that individual accountable will prevent more people from being positively impacted. These ideas – that certain special individuals connect us to God and must be looked to for us to hear from God – will be explored in this chapter. Both cause us to see these individuals as deserving of protection at all costs. They undermine our willingness to discern what is taking place, and call out the 'called'.

WORDS FROM GOD? CALLING, POWER AND SPEECH

Preaching projections

There are few things I enjoy as much as preaching. After becoming comfortable with reading Bible passages aloud in church services, my next step at 14 years old was to preach at a Sunday morning service as part of a summer youth mission in Birmingham. Revd Les Isaac asked me whether I would prepare a ten-minute sermon. I called it 'Where is the Church?' I remember standing at the front after feeling sick with nerves, and suddenly I felt fine, then more than fine. I asked a very profound theological question, for someone that young: where is the Church in relation to the mission God has given us? I knew even then that there was something sacred and holy about being trusted to stand in front of God's people and speak to them about what you believe will build them up in the faith. I feel the same awe over 20 years later.

Preaching is one of the most powerful opportunities a person has within a church. As we stand in the pulpit or walk around with a microphone, people attribute a certain amount of power to our words. This varies, of course – people did not give as much authority to my 14-year-old self as they would to Dr Selina Stone. And today some people will struggle to give the same authority to a preacher like me – an unmarried laywoman with a (slight) Brummie accent from a Pentecostal background – as they would to others. It matters, therefore, who we see regularly as preachers since we tend to assume that the person who is preaching is there because God has chosen or called them. This can be the case, but it is also true that much more goes into deciding who gets to preach than we might want to admit. Our collective biases, and politics, play out everywhere. If we looked across the board at preachers across traditions, we would find people end up in pulpits not solely (or even in any part) due to divine calling but for a range of other reasons. Maybe they have the right title, status or surname, they went to the right training college or university, or they have powerful allies in the institution. They might be there at least partly due to being considered attractive on some level, or because they present as straight, are neurotypical, have a certain accent or tone to their voice and any other number of factors. Since God shows no partiality, we can trust that it is not God who is biased, but us, in the preaching and preachers we value.

Many of us who preach will be aware of these dynamics and may seek to address them in some way. We might seek to downplay our power through self-deprecating jokes, but this simply pretends to equalize. We might share vulnerable stories, but again, this does not correct the power differential. It is, unfortunately, inevitable. No matter how much any of us might hope to communicate a certain level of humanity, humility or uncertainty, people will view us, though in different ways, as having power that should be respected and listened to. This is why we must vary the people we count as preachers and resist the urge to create cookie-cutter preaching styles which undermine variety and diverse perspectives on the biblical texts. To go even further, we might examine creative ways of forming meaning from Scripture that go beyond a single person being considered a divine vessel.

Preaching is a powerful mechanism for shaping minds. It deserves particular attention because of the way preaching is so often tied up in spiritual abuse and abuse of power.[2] The reality is that for those of us who are preachers, what is happening inside us so often leaks into sermons and what we say through a microphone when we are standing in front of a gathered group of people. For good or for evil. For those who are engaged in patterns of power abuse, preaching, in which they project certain theologies of power, is an important place to look for signs.

In this next section, I am going to reflect on aspects of a sermon preached by Mike Pilavachi at the School of Ministry at the Charismatic Catch the Fire church in Toronto in 2013 on the theme of insecurity.[3] Watching this sermon, which at the time of writing is available on YouTube, was chilling in light of what has now been alleged about Pilavachi's behaviour during the years of his ministry and even before. Reports started to emerge of coercive and abusive behaviour by Pilavachi during the years of his ministry at Soul Survivor Watford, a church he founded. In September 2023 an internal investigation by the Church of England found that Pilavachi 'used his spiritual authority to control people and that his coercive and controlling behaviour led to inappropriate relationships, the physical wrestling of youths and massaging of young male interns.'[4] Pilavachi is no longer able to minister in the Church, having resigned his ministry license to his bishop, and has also resigned from his role at Soul Survivor. In November 2023, Soul Survivor subsequently reported that the trustees had commissioned Fiona Scolding KC to conduct an independent review into the culture and practices of Soul Survivor.[5] The report published in September 2024 included important revelations about the dynamics of power at play at Soul Survivor. Mike Pilavachi is reported to have:

> made it clear that he did not believe that he had a special relationship with God and that his teaching sought to identify that everyone has a special relationship and that there is no hierarchy of who can hear God's voice.[6]

Yet, at the same time, reviewers conclude:

> The religious context is likely to have compounded [the] sense of wilful blindness. The success of the venture would have been attributed by many to God's favour, both on the movement and upon Mr Pilavachi. Someone who was perceived to have been favoured by God to that extent would have been even harder to challenge: to challenge Mr Pilavachi's approach was almost to challenge God's work.[7]

Clearly what was *stated*, and what was *embodied*, caused conflicting narratives which, in the end, resulted in Pilavachi's status as God's divine mouthpiece and sacred tool.

The purpose of analysing this sermon is not to present Pilavachi's preaching as a unique case. There are surely many questionable sermons given on a weekly basis, and some may well have come out of my own mouth. Few of us would want our sermons to be picked to pieces in hindsight, by those who became privy to our own failings. But the difference in a case like this is that when spiritual leaders abuse power, many aspects of their ministry are often tied up in that abuse. Preaching is a primary way of grooming a congregation as well as an individual. It is a strategy used – consciously or unconsciously – to prepare a person to be abused for spiritual reasons and to prepare a community to accept the abuse and defend the abuser if accusations eventually emerge. By presenting particular ideas of what God is like, how God works and who we are in relation, sermons are weaponized in ways that disempower the hearer and concentrate even more power in the mouth and hands of the preacher. It is also the case that by highlighting the theologies that enable abuse, we might also come to understand something of the concept of God such a person is living with. These theologies harm the listener but also the preacher. They reveal the abusive god often worshipped and diligently served by those in the pulpit. This is a god who demands never-ending sacrifice, self-mutilation and mistreatment as signs of faithfulness.

The sermon in question takes as its key text the story of Jacob's life from his deception of his twin Esau to their reconciliation, recalled in Genesis 25.19—33.20. Throughout this sermon, we can find some concerning ideas about the nature of God, Pilavachi's confessions of mean behaviour to his colleagues and some harsh interpretations of the figures in the text. He begins by asking the audience to choose what they want to hear: a talk on leadership or a talk on insecurity, and they vote, we presume, for the latter. The sermon begins with his reading parts of the story and then filling in the gaps by riffing on the read portions, in an engaging and spontaneous style. It is impressive and fun to listen to. But what lies beneath is a quite organized theological system, one that suggests mistreatment by another can be designed by God for your good. In addition, there is, in my view, a telling relationship between his vulnerable sharing about trauma and insecurity in his own life, his recognition that this is an ongoing problem and a simultaneous notion that he has been 'healed'.

Pilavachi's account of Jacob's life in this sermon is one marked by insecurity, which then leads to a life of deception. He discusses, first, the significance of Jacob being the younger twin and missing out on the cultural benefits of being the oldest. Then he goes on to comment on Jacob's masculinity, calling him 'a bit of a wuss' and 'a mummy's boy' in contrast to Esau, who was 'a man's man', interested in hunting and killing. Pilavachi reads Jacob's love for Rachel as something that renders him a 'pathetic man', driven by insecurity rather than deep affection, disparaging the thought that he would work seven additional years for Rachel's hand in marriage after he was tricked into marrying Leah. But overall Pilavachi emphasizes Jacob being a deceiver, as does the biblical text.

The unusual turn comes in his assertion that God set Jacob up with an exploitative and deceptive father-in-law to teach him a harsh lesson; in fact, to give him what he deserved: 'Jacob was an amazing deceiver, so what God did was he gave him as a gift, Laban, to be his father-in-law who was even more of a deceiver.' When all is said and done, and Jacob has been tricked into working for 14 years for Rachel whom he was promised he would have after seven years, Jacob, he argues, 'could have wasted time being furious at Laban, but ... he saw through the man's deception, God's chastising.' This, for Pilavachi, is a lesson that God, 'because he loves us', will sometimes bring what we might describe as 'toxic', manipulative or even abusive individuals into our lives. This, in Pilavachi's mind, is done 'in order to kill us' (a generous reading is to see this as meaning 'to kill' what might be the sinful aspects of us), to 'wind us up' or 'be an irritant'. It is not clear what this irritant or kind of death will achieve in his mind, but it is, for him, by divine design.

Exegetical preaching, in which we seek to derive meaning from the biblical texts for our contemporary lives, is a complicated business if done with any integrity. By this, I mean it is not straightforward if we recognize the complexity of the texts themselves, which have been compiled over centuries. In addition, we are faced with the lack of historical evidence for some of what is found within the texts, and our struggle to understand the contexts of some stories where we can trust they may actually have happened. This difficulty is felt even by the minority of us who have committed years to studying biblical texts. This is not to say we cannot get meaning from these stories by reflecting on them with a cup of tea and open hearts, but we must always be mindful of our possible projections into the text. In the case of this story of Jacob, I may have experienced much deception and mistreatment in my life, and in order to make sense of how or why God could or would allow this, I might begin to construct an idea of God, who in fact does want me to be in such situations for my good. I may read this into the biblical account, ignoring verses that declare that God leads us into green pastures, or that God is a good shepherd who only sends good shepherds and warns us about wolves who deceive, coming dressed as sheep.

I am not in a position to know how Pilavachi came to these interpretations of this biblical story. But what I am clear on is the way this idea, that God sends deceivers, exploiters and maybe even abusers into our lives, is highly problematic. This message undermines any instinct to complain against the 'Labans' or hold them to account. It gaslights those of us being exploited or unfairly treated by causing us to question whether God is somehow sanctioning it because of some fault in us. It causes us to think that those who abuse power may be being used by God and that we should focus on the potential spiritual effect of their actions rather than addressing their problematic behaviour.

The second aspect of this sermon that exemplifies the problematics of preaching power in churches relates to the way Pilavachi reflects theologically on his own insecurities. Pilavachi gives an account of what can only be described as a deeply traumatic experience of starting school in England, without being able to speak English. He recalls, in vivid detail, being dragged away from his mother, who promises to stay all day but leaves him, inevitably, and his feelings of abandonment. He then explains that he lived for two years withdrawn from close relationships, in relative silence, during which time he only uttered 'yes' or 'no' to essential questions. He describes suicidal thoughts, emotional and mental distress and extreme loneliness. In the midst of this he has a conversion experience, and on reflection declares that 'God began to heal me.'

Before we can think too highly of him as a 'healed' person, he jumps into a story about friends of his who confronted him about his mean behaviour towards his colleagues. They observed, he recalls, that whenever he returned from a trip he exhibited controlling unkind behaviour when he was back working with the team. They stated, 'We're almost all expecting it now.' He reflects on their words and recognizes what they describe is true. He then makes a connection to his childhood trauma:

> Then it suddenly hit me, I've been away on a trip and I come back and the gut feeling that's inside … is they've really enjoyed playing together without me. I'm back, they have to be nice to me, but none of them really want me. So I couldn't not turn up, it was my job, I was the pastor, so it was like … I'll show them who's in charge …

He goes on to explain that when he is tired or low he can sometimes succumb to those insecure thoughts. 'I still visit that place,' he says, 'but I don't live there anymore … God has healed me.' Many of us will be able to identify with the way childhood trauma can affect us during adulthood. It takes a certain amount of self-awareness to be able to notice the roots of behavioural patterns and habits, whether they are positive or negative. The confessing of our own limitations can be a bold act, in a context where people might assume we are perfect or have arrived at spiritual maturity. Being honest about our mistakes and the ways we fall short can do a lot to challenge the projections of congregants who demand a perfect preacher or leader, or can unconsciously put such a person on a pedestal no matter what they might do to resist it. But what strikes me here is the confidence with which he distances himself from his actual behaviour: 'I don't live there anymore.' This of course is a reference to being in a mental space of insecurity. In comparison to his childhood story where his insecurities were so severe that he was suicidal, it can be said he does not live *there* anymore. But his insecurities causing him to lash out at those in his care would suggest he is still living somewhere close to *there*. While his childhood self may have turned the violence inward, with no one else to turn it on, as an adult he has the power to act out his internal issues on others.

He spiritualizes this attempt to distance himself from abusive behaviour by claiming that God has healed him. This narrative effectively undermines any critical exploration of his behaviour – for questioning his healing may feel as if one is questioning God. Who can say a person is not healed, if they say they are? Well, in this case, it would be those living at the receiving end of his ministry. Whether or not insecurity could be held responsible – and I am no psychoanalyst – it would seem that this same playground logic was evident in many places. Those who have given testimony of their experiences of abusive behaviour at the hands of Pilavachi have described certain games. Some spoke of being picked out and pulled close into an 'inner circle' and then being immediately pushed away and ostracized with no explanation.[8] According to these testimonies, his 'mean' behaviour was not a one-off, corrected after his friends brought it to his attention, but a pattern of behaviour over many years. Some women in romantic relationships with his 'chosen ones' – who were all young men – felt his resentment, especially as their relationships became serious and the couples planned to marry.⁹ This could have been underpinned by a lack of appreciation for the dynamics of heterosexual relationships, seen in his harsh (I would argue mis-) reading of the 'pathetic' Jacob who fell in love with Rachel.

The case of Mike Pilavachi is a devastating one, and as we have seen, we must be mindful of how the preaching we offer or hear can reveal hidden theologies which groom people to accept abuse. This is not always deliberate, nor is it always conscious. As preachers, we preach the God we know. The same harmful theologies and perspectives we might offer to others are often the ones that cage and haunt our daily lives. The question remains of what harm might have been avoided, if these ideas about God and God's ways with us, might have been explored with a spiritual guide and challenged in a gracious manner. I wonder if such an intervention might have enabled him to discover a kindness in God, that may have helped soothe the childhood wounds that he described so openly, helping him to be a kinder presence to those around him. It is for the sake of the preacher and those who listen, that these theological and spiritual issues must be addressed. This particular example should compel us to understand to a greater degree the importance of pastoral theological training – that is, training in theology that makes links with the pastoral issues people face and the care they need. But it should also motivate us to take even greater care, as we reflect on the power of preaching, for good and for ill.

Having our say: The power of the tongue

In his 1987 book, *The Mighty from their Thrones: Power in the Biblical Tradition*, biblical scholar James P.M. Walsh provides an illuminating definition of power in the Hebrew Bible. Power is in part about 'having the say'.[10] While the author admits this is a slightly clumsy phrase, it is for Walsh the best way to translate the Hebrew word *mišpāt*. God's *mišpāt* can also be translated as 'judgement', 'authority' or 'rule', but Walsh considers them too narrow and laden with baggage.[11] First of all, it is God's *mišpāt*, 'God having God's say', that governs the world. And out of God's generosity, God's *mišpāt* allows us as human beings the capacity to have our own *mišpāt* through which we make our voice heard, and also negotiate with others and their *mišpāt*. Walsh explains divine *mišpāt* in the Hebrew Bible as crucial, meaning dread for 'the wicked and for the nations' but consolation and liberation for 'the just'.[12] God having God's say sets boundaries for humanity; it allows us to understand what to see as right or wrong, what we should accept and resist. In other words, it helps us see how to use our own power or *mišpāt*.

Intent on resisting the way that the Old and New Testaments can be opposed to each other, Walsh stresses the continuity between the two, explaining that for the Early Christians, Jesus was understood as the one in and through whom 'the *mišpāt* of Yahweh became a reality.'[13] Jesus is understood, for the Early Christians, to be the full embodiment of divine *mišpāt*. He is the living word, God having God's say completely and finally. Jesus' actions of healing and exorcism are, for Walsh, exhibitions of divine *mišpāt*, as are his teachings, sermons and parables:

> Many of [the parables] answer the question about Yahweh's *mišpāt*. How does God rule the world? Where is the evidence that he is involved in any way whatever? When can we expect to see his *mišpāt*? And the answer comes in images and in stories. God's *mišpāt* is like a seed: a seed is planted and it grows; you do not see it growing, you cannot track its growth, but it yields a miraculous harvest. God's *mišpāt* is hidden, but efficacious.[14]

This notion of power as 'having one's say' will resonate with us in terms of our experiences of powerlessness or what we think about healthy relationships. If we know what it is like not to have a say, or we know what kind of evils are possible when some groups do not get to have a say, then we have stumbled upon a fair example of why *mišpāt*, when defined in this way, has a lot to do with power. But this is also compelling when we think back to our initial discussion of power as divine breath, as seen in the creation stories of Genesis. God's breath gives life to humanity, enabling us to exist and to create through the power of this breath becoming our own even while it remains God's. If power is 'having the say', God's power is again the beginning, the source, the one that comes first. God has the *first* say with the words 'Let there be.' God expresses desire, creates out of divine imagination, and takes care to set spaces for flourishing and appropriate boundaries. The sea cannot go wherever it wants; it needs to be restrained lest it destroy everything else with its might. The animals need their opportunity to thrive, so the humans are commanded to eat only vegetation; they are nurtured, and they are also given limits. And when the eternal Word is born in flesh, and dwells among us, we see this continuation. God continues to have God's say in every word and action of Jesus. And God ultimately has the final say over sin and death itself, through the Resurrection. Whatever the principalities and powers might have *said*, in contradiction to the 'saying' of God, is overcome, defeated and rendered obsolete.

But of course, what we experience so often are realities and worlds created by the words of others and even our own, which do not align with God's sayings. We are bombarded by the sayings that come to us from our social and cultural norms, our political conversations, our church communities and friendships, our families and even random strangers on the internet. These words, like seeds, can go deep into the soil of our minds and hearts unnoticed, until they produce a shoot, a plant, then a tree and finally fruit. Fruit that we will consume, as will those around us. When the fruit is good, nurturing and rejuvenation take place. When the fruit is rotten, we are poisoned until we uproot the tree. The power of saying – whether we or others are the speakers – cannot be underestimated in our analysis of power, especially as we reflect on abuses of power in the Church.

The beauty of the Charismatic movement is in the expectation that anyone can receive the Spirit and the anointing, as well as the vocations the Spirit is believed to give for the sake of the Church's ministry. I knew this as a child, both because of the teaching in my church and my own spiritual experiences of receiving knowledge I did not naturally attain. We often called this 'receiving a word'. While I, as a girl in a classical Pentecostal church, held the Bible at the centre of my life of faith, we also believed that the Holy Spirit would speak to us, through Scripture but also in direct reference to the details of our lives. People clamoured to go to the front to be prayed for, with hope that a person who was in tune with the Spirit might share a word with them and remind them that God had heard and God was near. In my church, this was not something just anyone was allowed to do. People had to be trained to understand the power of these gifts and to steward them with care and caution. We knew that the voice of God would always encourage and 'edify' the hearer, so we should disregard any 'word' that would shame, judge or condemn someone – that was probably us, not God. And we knew also that we should not presume we had got it right, but also caveat that what we shared was only what we had felt or thought. The hearer, I was taught, also had the responsibility to 'weigh' the word and 'try' or 'test' the spirit. They should take it away and meditate and pray on it, thinking about their own journey of faith and how God has been speaking to them already. As my parents always said, 'God will tell you first, whatever anyone else says should only be confirmation.' I have disregarded many 'words' in my time because of this wise counsel.

One of my best stories of this is from my time at a Pentecostal Bible college. There was a particular church leader who had come as a guest speaker at some point during the year. He was a church planter with a strong vision for building large churches around the country. In the last few months of the year, he would come back to hover around, in an attempt to recruit the 'talent' for his enterprise. At this particular chapel service he preached and invited people up to the altar for prayer; I went up enthusiastically as I was having a hard time. He began to pray. The first thing he said – which was common at the time once people knew I wasn't married – was that God had a husband for me. And he then asked me a series of questions about what I was planning to do after Bible college, to which I replied, 'I do not know.' The next 'word' he gave me was that he saw a picture of me kneeling down and washing the feet of a man of God. That as I served this man faithfully, God would make space for my own calling. It took me a while to realize he probably meant himself, as the following year he circled back to have a conversation about God's calling on my life. I passed.

When I recall this story, of a white Evangelical man in his 40s having this vision of a Black woman in her 20s, I really do think how gracious God was to him that I did not know better. I do not think I was singled out, I am sure he had this 'word' for many other people regardless of gender or race, but my womanist senses tingle when I think back to it now. I held this word in my mind for several years as I navigated life, family and career goals. Every now and then I would have a male boss, and wonder, 'Was this the man?' But in the end, I let it go. And I have found my path to my calling quite well without needing to wash a man's feet, thankfully.

I realize I am privileged to have had parents and pastors who could help me navigate the minefield of charismatic gifts. I was taught to be cautious but not cynical, and it has served me well. But what we have seen in countless stories of abuse in the church is the power of words, which goes unacknowledged, and a lack of teaching about how to handle the power that comes with spiritual expressions. This power does not just affect the spiritual life; it affects emotional and mental health, and psychological and material well-being. Whether words said 'in jest', preaching or 'prophetic words', language is at the core of so many of these stories of power abuse. This is especially the case in Charismatic settings which value words so much more than silence. But even in spaces that we might imagine to be safer, liturgies can hold incredible power in shaping our theological imaginations. 'Life and death' are revealed to be 'in the power of the tongue' wherever we might find ourselves.

Whose 'say' are we missing?

I grew up in Birmingham, near the Black Country. This area is so named not because it's full of Black people (which is what I initially thought it meant as a child, when on my way to the Black Country Museum on a primary school trip) but because of the historic coal mines. Coal mining represented an important industry in the UK from the Industrial Revolution onwards. For over two centuries, generations of British workers risked and lost life and health working down the mines to provide energy for the country. To be a coal miner was more than a job; it brought a sense of pride, identity and security to countless working-class families and the towns that sprang up around the mines. But with it came the danger of death, due to the release of poisonous gases like carbon monoxide that could kill humans and animals. Coal miners in Britain and elsewhere would take two caged canaries with them down into the mines, since they were far more sensitive than humans and could detect poisonous gas 100 times quicker. If a canary got sick or collapsed and died, the miners would know to rush out of the mine to the fresh air. This practice thankfully ended when machine detectors were invented.

In thinking about the way theology can contribute to abuse in churches, I am reminded of the canaries, as I think of those people who signal to us early on that something might be wrong. It happens, I think, in stories we have heard of scandals in big churches. There are always people who act as canaries

WORDS FROM GOD? CALLING, POWER AND SPEECH

in the mine. Usually, they are the 'little people' who are considered annoying. It might be the woman who 'won't let it go', the older person who 'keeps going on', or the insightful individual who 'nitpicks' about things that seem insignificant to the people in charge. Their screeches and wing flapping are ignored, and the gas seeps in. They are considered distractions from the important work and are sidelined for not being on board with the vision – but their complaints could save lives, at least spiritually.

But the sad thing is that we often wait until certain kinds of people are negatively impacted before we take note. The canaries die one after another, and we roll our eyes and mutter, 'What on earth is wrong with them? Where is their resilience?' And we keep on mining. I will admit to feeling triggered when I have seen some footage about the kinds of abusive behaviour in the Church that revolve around access to leaders or the stage. Usually, it is a white, middle-class married person or couple on the screen. One or both of them might be crying about what has happened to them. They used to be the beloved, at the centre of things, and now they find themselves on the margins. I feel a measure of empathy. They go on to say that they were preaching all the time, invited to all the special dinners, and brought right up close to the person in power, only to be cast aside the first time they made a tiny mistake or a big one. Suddenly they realized they were not as special or as chosen as they thought they were. They imagined they were top of a hierarchy of favour, and they were flung to the bottom – or so it feels – and they describe the depths of their devastation.

I am not going to belittle these accounts of the pain of falling out of favour. This is of course a painful thing for anyone. But I will admit that as someone who would never have the kind of access to power they have had, I struggle to empathize fully. In Christian contexts where white married couples occupy the highest rungs of power, there are tons of people who from the outset are treated as not quite enough. There is no ejection from the inner circle because we would never be permitted to enter it to start with. In some cases, these couples or individuals have helped to build and sustain an abusive structure and culture for years, and have gained all the benefits. The most notable case of this is the Carl Lentz fiasco at Hillsong New York. Watching the documentary *The Secrets of Hillsong* was the first time I felt this frustration.[15] As Lentz cried on screen about him being removed from his position and almost losing his family through his own actions, I asked myself how to respond to someone who enabled the abusive and exploitative dynamics he was now complaining about. Now that he had been bitten by the monster he created, it seemed to me he wanted us all to stop and weep with him. It emerged throughout the documentary that people from minoritized ethnic groups were experiencing forms of mistreatment, young socio-economically vulnerable people were being exploited, and those who identified as queer were marginalized. These were canaries in the mine, fighting to be heard, and fighting to live. But they were not heard, and the environment continued to become toxic. In the UK, it has taken the courage of Matt and Beth Redman who produced a documentary about their experiences with Mike Pilavachi to provoke minor actions by some who remained silent during months of stories and investigations because of their friendship with and platforming of Pilavachi. The canaries chirped, then screeched, and the shovelling continued. Each week Natalie Collins updated her live report on X and her *God Loves Women* blog with more stories, accusations and testimonies, and still, silence.[16] These voices did not warrant a response. They were unvalued, untrusted and easily overlooked. Even by leaders in churches. An anonymous guest post was shared on Natalie Collins's blog on 16 April 2024 by two people who reported their abuse by Pilavachi. It is entitled 'Overturn the Tables'. I end with an extended quotation but the whole post is worth reading:

> Almost 150 people, with varying degrees of power and status in relation to Christian communities, have now stepped

forward to share personal experiences of abuse at the hands of Mike Pilavachi and Soul Survivor. The public response from those considered to be 'leaders' within these communities has been mixed. Some have chosen to remain silent; others have spoken a little here and there, being careful not to appear overly critical of their friends or those in high places; still others have expressed support for Mike Pilavachi. Those vocal in their support of victims and others impacted by events have been in the minority.

Until the release of Matt and Beth Redman's documentary this week.

At the root of this week's sudden flurry of activity among 'leaders', and underlying their response to the public revelation of Mike Pilavachi's abuse more generally, seems to us to be the market logic that permeates our Christian communities ... And under this logic, all bodies – including the bodies of the abused – appear not as temples of the Holy Spirit, but as commodities to be valued or disposed of ... [the market logic] is perpetuating the abuse we ourselves experienced through Soul Survivor, where we were not treated with dignity and worth, and where our suffering – which is now being used by others for personal and institutional gain – was not seen as being of equal importance to sustaining Mike's 'ministry'.[17]

It begins and ends: 'Overturn your tables, pour out your coins, Stop making these temples marketplaces!'
Selah.

Notes

1 Lisa Oakley and Justin Humphreys, *Escaping the Maze of Spiritual Abuse: Creating Healthy Christian Cultures* (London: SPCK, 2019), p. 58.
2 Lisa Oakley and Kathryn Kinmond, *Breaking the Silence on Spiritual Abuse* (London Palgrave Macmillan, 2013), p. 46.
3 Catch the Fire Toronto, 'E/F: Insecurity (Mike Pilavachi at the

SoM) Mike Pilavachi', *YouTube* (16 September 2012), https://www.youtube.com/watch?v=PbxA5YO201E (accessed 23.05.2024).

4 The Church of England, 'Concerns Substantiated in Mike Pilavachi Investigation', *Church of England*, 6 September 2023, https://www.churchofengland.org/media/press-releases/concerns-substantiated-mike-pilavachi-investigation (accessed 10.12.2024).

5 Soul Survivor, 'Launch of Independent Review', 21 November 2023, https://www.soulsurvivorwatford.co.uk/latestupdates (accessed 10.12.2024).

6 Fiona Scolding KC and Ben Fullbrook, 'Independent Review into Soul Survivor', 26 September 2024, p. 49, https://www.soulsurvivorwatford.co.uk/outcome (accessed 3.12.2024).

7 Scolding and Fullbrook, 'Independent Review', p. 79.

8 Soul Survivors Podcast, 'Episode 3: The Open Secret', *Premier Christianity*, 23 February 2024, https://www.premier.plus/soul-survivors/podcasts/soul-survivors/episode-3-the-open-secret (accessed 3.12.2024); Matt and Beth Redman, 'Let There be Light', *YouTube*, 9 April 2024, https://www.youtube.com/watch?v=YVZkgdt32u8&t=36s (accessed 3.12.2024).

9 Soul Survivors Podcast, 'Episode 3: The Open Secret'; Matt and Beth Redman, 'Let There Be Light'.

10 J.P.M. Walsh, *The Mighty from their Thrones: Power in the Biblical Tradition* (Philadelphia, PA: Fortress Press, 1987), p. 3.

11 Walsh, *The Mighty from their Thrones*, p. 4.

12 Walsh, *The Mighty from their Thrones*, p. 148.

13 Walsh, *The Mighty from their Thrones*, p. 149.

14 Walsh, *The Mighty from their Thrones*, p. 167.

15 *The Secrets of Hillsong* is a four-part documentary by FX Networks about a history of cover-ups in Hillsong Church, which began in Australia. It revolves around the removal of Carl Lentz as senior pastor of Hillsong New York in 2020, after his extramarital affair became public knowledge. It then recalls the history of the church network, including the cover-up of child sexual abuse by the founder Brian Houston. At the time of writing it is available on Disney+ in the UK.

16 Natalie Collins, *God Loves Women* blog, https://mrsglw.wordpress.com/ (accessed 3.12.2024); 'Needs Light', X.com, https://x.com/needs_light (accessed 3.12.2024).

17 Natalie Collins, 'Guest Post: Overturn the Tables', *God Loves Women* blog, 16 April 2024 (accessed 2.07.2024).

3

The Almighty: Power, Our Work and God's Ways

In this chapter, I explore some significant questions, some of which might feel scary because they destabilize what many of us have taken for granted without thinking them through. But it is important to me, as someone raised to take the Bible, God and the life I live seriously, that we are honest about the complexities and incongruencies that exist in some of our beliefs and practices. One such complexity emerges when we speak about the power of God, and most notably when we speak about God as all-powerful or almighty. Wherever you find yourself on the spectrum of Christian theology, the power of God features highly in one way or another. It is sung and preached about; it is the basis of our intercessions, and core to our liturgies. In an eagerness to encourage people in their faith we focus on displays of power in the Bible, as opposed to what we could read as God's inaction. We, for example, name God a liberator because of the exodus, and ignore (or at least downplay) the 400 years of silence and inaction despite the generations of cries and tears. I understand why, but I question it. Rarely is God's power explored or examined with honesty.

At the same time, when we face crises personally or collectively the almightiness of God can be the first theological assumption that we call into question when we cry out, 'Why would God let this happen?' Yes, in part, as experts in theodicy will explain, it is a question about why we suffer, and how a loving God could allow us to suffer. But it is also a question about God's power. Why, if God is able to do all things, has God not done what we deem is necessary? Or how has God not prevented what apparently stands against his will and intentions? It is the first question I asked as a child growing up in the inner city, and in a Pentecostal church which gave me a very high view of divine power: if God is powerful and able to do (or undo) all things, then why is life not changing for us? Why, with all the churches' and all of our prayers, does God not do anything about the lack of opportunities, lack of hope, poverty and desperation so many people face?

We can at times turn back on ourselves to find answers. Maybe we have failed somehow in our prayers or actions. The importance of our agency, decision making and action should not be downplayed of course. But if I may, the question should be thrown back to theology, to those of us who preach and teach – have we misunderstood divine power? What are the ethical, practical consequences of the particular emphases we have chosen, and what might offer a helpful counterbalance?

The idea that God is almighty – the ultimate being with the capacity and moral authority to do whatever God wants – has important consequences for abuses of power. This is because almightiness is a seductive concept that some (maybe all of us) are tempted to desire for ourselves. But it is also dangerous because, though calling God almighty, we have also sought ways to explain away Almighty God's inaction in light of pain, suffering and abuse. If God can be 'let off the hook' through theological contortions which make God ultimately responsible and also not, then this, I fear, is projected on to individuals and institutions that on the one hand have huge power in their contexts, and on the other normalize not acting to care for those who experience abuse. While the solution may lie, for some, in simply blaming humans for not using their power as they should – which is a fair point in many cases – I instead want to focus on rethinking God's power, especially in relation to ideas about how God works and what God is or is not doing.

Almightiness, when not properly examined, risks seducing us to worship idols without us knowing. We begin to look at demonstrations of power, of dominance, of growth, and assume this is the work of God, especially when Christian language and symbols are utilized. We follow this illusion, sacrificing precious things on the altar of this idol, imagining somehow that we are serving the living God. We give our best to protect this work, to defend the sacrifices no matter how extreme. Nothing is too sacred to be killed, no blood too innocent to be poured out. What can rescue us from this deception? It is to these questions that we turn in this chapter.

God: The Almighty and his servants

To be almighty is to have power that others do not have, and thus to enact your will, in spite of opposition, which is not opposition in any real sense since nothing can truly oppose you. This is the power that we tend to ascribe to God.[1] God is 'God all by himself', as Black preachers like to shout.[2] He has no need of others, is accountable to none but himself. But, we are told, we have no need to fear this power, for it is defined by love, and is ultimately for our own good. Since we as human beings are sinful, flawed and inherently self-centred, it is best for us to submit to God's good power for our sakes and for the sake of all. The power we have is allowed by God to fulfil certain functions and should be modelled after God as loving power. God does not lose power by giving us power – power is not a zero-sum game – but God allows us to exert power that is always his. The power given by God to human beings, to govern the world God made in Genesis, forms the basis of this understanding of the relationship between divine and human power.

But the question of God and power, particularly almightiness, has caused something of a conundrum for theologians who have felt the effects of what almightiness can do in actual human experience. For German theologians witnessing and reflecting on the rise of the Nazis in Germany, power and almightiness became important themes for reflection. In one of Karl Barth's earlier and shorter writings, *Dogmatics in Outline*, he takes on the question of almightiness, in light of Hitler's claiming of the word:

> Perhaps you recall how, when Hitler used to speak about God, he called him 'the Almighty'. But it is not 'the Almighty' who is God; we cannot understand from the standpoint of a supreme concept of power, who God is. And the man who calls 'the Almighty' God misses God in the most terrible way. For 'the Almighty' is bad as 'power in itself' is bad. The 'Almighty' means chaos, evil, the devil. We could not better describe and define the devil than by trying to think this idea of a self-based, free, sovereign ability.[3]

Barth is concerned, in this whole discussion of divine power, with how we project our human experiences of understandings of power on to God in order to attempt to understand the One we cannot grasp. So we look around for examples of almightiness, or 'power in itself', as Hitler does, and we think, well, that must be what it means to speak of God as almighty. But for Barth, this kind of power actually undermines possibility. God's power properly understood is 'the essence of the possible', whereas almightiness is 'the end of all things'.[4] Everything that exists and lives does so because of God's being and God's power which is love itself, holy, kind, patient and righteous. But what is almighty suffocates.

I understand why this will jar with some of us. The idea of an almighty loving God is comforting, because when we recognize the end of our power, we can trust that there is a power that has things covered. And I do not necessarily believe that rethinking almightiness means God has no power at all. As I have said, divine power should, in my view, be understood primarily as breath, bringing life which is deeply powerful. Breath, *ruach*, or spirit is possibility, rather than a force weighing down, which is what almightiness suggests. It is almightiness which, when not properly interrogated, deceives us. It is the temptation Jesus faced when the devil promised him 'all authority [or power]' if he would bow down and worship him (Luke 4.6). It leads to the kind of thinking and practices that undermine and end possibility in so many ways, even while promising the opposite.

There is a story my siblings and I like to recall when we are remembering the top dramatic moments of our church childhoods. These are usually hilarious or shocking stories, which are seared into our memories from our younger years. They would make it into any high-quality church drama. One of my favourites is the story of the American 'prophet' (the reason for my use of quotation marks here will soon become clear) who came to town. In those days our church was full to the brim on a Sunday morning, and on a Sunday evening when we had a special guest. And an American prophet was the kind of guest people came out to see, even after a full Sunday morning programme. On this day, the prophet was, in typical American fashion, a rather round man with a very well-tailored and expensive suit. He was not wearing an extravagant watch but his shoes were made, it seemed to me, from some poor animal whose skin was now made extraordinarily shiny. In the first service, he soon began to demonstrate what everyone assumed at that point was a genuine gift of the 'word of knowledge'. In Charismatic churches, it is common for the spiritual gifts described by Paul in 1 Corinthians 12 to be exhibited. One of these is what the New King James Version calls 'the word of knowledge', interpreted in varying ways, but generally involving the receiving of knowledge via the Holy Spirit that a person has not learnt in any natural way.[5] In this case, the 'prophet' seemed to be able to tell people their name or address without them having met before. However, it turned out that he would take an offering, holding a bucket himself, and was reading the envelopes to garner this information, which he then used to pretend he had this gift. Our pastor noticed what he was doing, ended the service midway through and sent everyone but the church elders home. They gathered to deal with the charlatan in the church office. He admitted it, seeing no issue, and claimed, 'I was doing it to build up their faith.' He also hoped to encourage greater generosity in the second collection of tithes and offerings.

This incident of the American 'prophet' struck me, even as a young person, as a confession of a lack of faith. Not content with the form of power God sought to display or not, he decided to take matters into his own hands. Convinced that God *should* be impressive by displaying particular power, this time through divine knowledge, he conjured up an illusion that he hoped would sustain a particular understanding of God's power and intervention. When confronted, he believed he was working in tandem with God, that the ends justified the means, and his deception was acceptable because it was for (what he decided was) a worthy cause. Though we tell this story with humour these days, in more serious cases, the almighty leader who is believed to be anointed and empowered by almighty God can be a menacing figure. Such a person may in part be a victim of the projections of others, that they then feel they must live up to. It is clear to me that we are often, in small and large ways, complicit in creating such figures. Someone has to recommend them as speakers, others might have circulated recordings of their mighty acts, and expectation increases. Soon enough, they are primed to take advantage of those who have helped place them in a seat of great power. Even with the best intentions, the dynamic – whether the leader has contributed to their situation directly or attempted to avoid it – tempts leaders to maintain their position with displays of power worthy of the God they imagine. Katelyn Beaty explains it this way in *Celebrities for Jesus: How Personas, Platforms and Profits are Hurting the Church*:

> Few people go into ministry or leadership thinking they'll become tyrants, of course. It often starts with good motives. Someone with clear gifts and passion starts out wanting to leave a profound kingdom impact. They publicly embrace

the concept of servant leadership. They sincerely commit to external accountability. They seek to bless others instead of dominate them ... Then, at some point, maybe a leader feels what it's like to be treated like the most important person in the room. For a hush to fall over a crowd when they walk through the door. For people to hang on their every word. It feels good. Perhaps their followers and supporters tell them they have special, indispensable gifts and that God has destined them and their ministry for kingdom greatness. That also feels good. If they are impressive communicators who can captivate a crowd, it's likely that they start getting invited to speak and teach across the country. Their platform grows. It seems like God is expanding their reach ...[6]

The temptation of almightiness grows with the 'success' of ministry and expansion of influence, it would appear. What strikes me about this very good summary of what can often go wrong is the final statement – 'it *seems* that God is expanding their reach.' This is the crux of the problem for me: the ideas we have about how God's power relates to ours, in the context of ministry. We can, in some corners of the church, imagine that the godly thing to do is to claim that God is responsible for the growth or success we see. A church opens a new congregation, a project has a ton of money invested and we look at that, the *might* of it, and we assume it must be God. We see a person elevated to a position and we immediately speak as if God has chosen to put that person in that position. But what if we made a more honest assessment of how this success has actually happened? What if we admitted that this church movement is expanded because of wealthy donors dedicated to committing huge sums of money to pushing a particular brand of Christianity? What if we told the truth, that the person who was picked for that job is not there because God singled them out, but because they went to university with the decision makers, or have spent years rubbing shoulders with the 'right people' and proving themselves to be one of them?

It is a particular kind of blasphemy, I think, to claim boldly that God has done something that God may have little or nothing to do with, and yet I find we do this repeatedly without fear. In order to add weight to the decision that has been made, and to stifle questions or dissent, people speak as if God has ordained this as such. But at the same time, we may struggle to accept the mixed motives and interweaving forms of power that can be witnessed in places where abuse has happened. The dominating leader, as Katelyn describes, may have started off with good motives, and some of those kernels of good intentions may well remain. But there is also a desire to be liked, to be influential and to create something just how they want it. At their best, they may succeed in managing those less admirable instincts, but at their worst, they take the lead. So too, it can be that in spaces where abuse has taken place, individuals may have had experiences of God that have been life-changing in a good way. The same leader who mistreats and harms can also be kind and supportive at other times. The important thing, I think, is to free ourselves to tell the truth about what is happening and how, by resisting the urge to label everything that seems 'successful' as the work of God. Contrary to the capitalistic logics that dominate our global imagination and structures, huge numbers, expansion and growth do not always signal the good.

Exploitation in the name of the Almighty: The case of SPAC Nation

SPAC Nation (formally Salvation Proclaimer Ministries Limited) emerged seemingly out of thin air in London in around 2012. It was set up as a charity, then became a private limited company with the nature of its business including 'activities of religious organisations'. Its stated purpose was to help vulnerable young people and offenders, and this is in part what it became known for initially. The church was predominantly made up of young people and young adults, all led by Nigerian 'pastor' Tobi Adegboyega. His brother Adedapo Adegboyega also had a senior role. The congregation comprised many Black young people and notably appealed to young men who had been or were involved in criminality. Stories circulated about weapons being left at the altar, and conversions of young people and many others considered 'hard to reach'. Testimonies emerged about lives transformed. Young men in particular who were marginalized by wider British society were believed to be finding a spiritual home but also a network for developing a positive future for themselves. Rumours circulated that young men were leaving gangs and starting businesses and helping fund God's work through their entrepreneurial skills.[7] On the surface, it seemed to be an extraordinary work of God, and an answer to what inner city London needed.

But the apparent good and even godly work of SPAC Nation acted as a cover for a culture of exploitation and abuse. At first, whispers could be heard about the financial manipulation of young people. This soon became a cacophony in 2019. The Charity Commission launched a statutory inquiry into SPAC Nation which was announced in December 2019.[8] Nadine White and Emma Youle at the *Huffington Post* published several key articles after investigating the stories themselves.[9] They uncovered a culture of no accountability for leaders, in which rogue pastors could rise to prominence and exploit young people. This included financial exploitation – including coercing people to sell blood and give the payment to the church, nicknamed 'bleeding for seed'. There was also at least one case of alleged sexual assault in a house set up by leaders at the church for young people to live in.[10] One of the most well-known leaders at SPAC Nation was Mariam Mbula, and a BBC Three documentary was made about her career as a scam artist.[11] She was appointed as a leader over some of the housing projects, despite her many years of experience in fraud, for which she has been convicted in Belgium, Spain and the UK. In one now infamous video, Vic Santoro, a UK rapper, took to

Instagram to share a story of his little brother being coerced into giving his personal financial details to pastors. According to Santoro, Tobi and two other 'pastors' met with his brother to assure him all was well, and proceeded to register a business at his mum's house, where his brother lived. The pastors then set up a business account and withdrew the full £2,000 overdraft, leaving the debt in his brother's name.[12] BBC Panorama created a special episode about SPAC Nation entitled 'Conned by my Church', which first aired on 16 December 2019.[13] A Met Police investigation was launched, but no charges were filed against the church, only individuals, and the investigation was then dropped in 2020.[14] The BBC reported that the organization was wound up by the High Court in 2022 due to suspicious and incorrect accounts.[15]

The church was the subject of parliamentary debate raised by Steve Reed, the Labour MP for Croydon North, in January 2020.[16] In Hansard (the written record of the parliamentary debate) we find an account of the stories Steve Reed heard in the two days it took him to call back those who got in touch after he tweeted about his concerns. The pattern he recalls is that young people from poorer parts of London were groomed through gifts and meals, and brought into an inner circle:

> Then, what appears to be brainwashing starts. They are told that if their life is unsuccessful, if their family is poor, that is because they are not giving enough money to God. They call it seed: 'If you give seed to God – as much as you can lay your hands on – you will become rich.' This is the message they try to pump into these young people's heads. The organisation's leaders display extraordinary wealth. They drive cars worth hundreds of thousands of pounds. They wear Rolex watches and expensive designer suits, and they live in multimillion-pound properties. All of this is way beyond the experience of the young people they are targeting. They tell these vulnerable young people that they became rich by giving seed to God and tell them that they can have the same, but first they

have to give, and by any means possible ... One young victim told me they had prayer sessions, which she described as brainwashing, for up to eight hours a day, but the emphasis was not on God or spirituality; it was on wealth and money and the need to give seed to God in order to get rich.[17]

According to the testimonies Steve Reed heard from many callers, the young people were then encouraged to commit fraud and hand the money to the church. They handed over student loans and then got into serious debt trying to stay at university, and in some cases could not. Sometimes the pastors used details without the person's permission. Another MP, Siobhain McDonagh, who served the constituency of Mitcham and Morden, shares a heartbreaking local story:

> On SPAC Nation and the financial implications of some of its dealings, my Hon. Friend will be aware of the case of the late Mrs Osinlaru, who seems to have obtained a £150,000 secured loan on her house. Tragically she passed away, leaving her two young adult daughters and 13-year-old son in the house, unaware of this control over it. The house was later repossessed and a bailiff's warrant secured, but that was stopped only because of the presence of the young 13-year-old son. That family risk losing their home and becoming homeless because of a loan they did not know about, and their mum has passed away. I have written to the church and it has admitted that it was involved in securing, or helping to secure, that loan.[18]

Reports of the behaviour of 'pastors' at SPAC Nation measure up against any definition of spiritual abuse. The core financial elements are compounded by the psychological and physical abuse of coercing young people to the point that they would sell their blood. The themes of blood, suffering and sacrifice will be addressed in detail in Chapter 5. Suffice to say at this point that when it comes to abuse, destructive creativity knows no bounds.

In the case of SPAC Nation, we find a culture of abuse, developed in large part due to the love of money that had taken over the organization's architects. The church had no building, instead meeting in luxury hotels around London. Pastors dressed in designer clothes, wore Rolex watches and drove fancy cars. They sought to present an image of economic power and success to young people in the inner city, many of whom were vulnerable and lived with financial need. They used wealth to groom young people, recruiting them in their usual hangout spots and giving them phones and watches, before exploiting them for financial gain. To put this in more explicit theological terms, SPAC Nation, if they believed in God at all, believed in a god who was almighty and required them to be almighty in the lives of the young people they exploited. They promised them a god who could give them unlimited wealth and they sought to embody this. They projected a god who had the power to house or unhouse them, to place them in luxury and even to bring them to a meeting at the prime minister's office. This god demanded everything from those who had little. Almightiness here truly represented 'the end of possibilities' for so many of the young people left in the wake of this predatory organization.[19]

Though the emphasis on spiritual abuse is financial in this example and feels extreme, it is important for us to recognize the subtle ways in which the labour and exploitation of congregations and volunteers can be abused to prop up individuals and institutions in unjust ways. For the record, I am not against people being encouraged to give to cover the costs of the churches they belong to or benefit from, or to support organizations doing work they value and want to see continue. Nor am I suggesting people should simply attend and consume, especially from a church, without seeking ways to offer out of their capacity so others can also be supported. But it is all too easy for people to feel or be told they cannot say no to the almighty leader. This is especially the case when Scripture is used to guilt-trip people into giving. Lisa Oakley explains one testimony of a respondent in her research on spiritual abuse:

> Every time he wanted me to do something, he would quote scripture. Sometimes it would be about sacrifice if he wanted me to give more time to the church. Sometimes it was about obedience if I was asking a question about something I was uncomfortable with. It was really difficult to argue, I couldn't argue with scripture, it was like I was arguing with God. I felt under more and more pressure.[20]

The increasing pressure to give is a common example of what can happen in settings where the leader has a vision that is far beyond the capacity of themselves and the people they are leading. Some may imagine that this is the nature of faith-filled leadership, to have something to reach for together. This can be true, but wisdom must be applied to discerning what is driving this vision: is it the individual fantasies or ego needs of the person or people in charge? Or at least some level of reflective dialogue with all those who have a stake in what will be proposed? What capacity is there for things to be slowed down, or plans to be scrapped if those responsible for making it happen are overworked or tired, or have major concerns? A capitalistic logic, in service of the almighty, must push on regardless, like a bus speeding along through red lights. There is no time for questions, queries or concerns, simply a determination to get to the destination as quickly as possible, even if only a handful have survived the journey. As I say, this is born, in part, out of a sense of us serving a god who is most concerned about productivity, efficiency and speed. This pragmatic god has no interest in 'the little people', simply the will and desires of 'the anointed' and 'the called'.

The widow's mite/might

This question of almightiness and the exploitation of the vulnerable has economic and also class dynamics to it, as we see in the case of SPAC Nation. Anyone can be abused financially in a religious setting of course, and there is a case to be made for considering how the wealthy can be dehumanized because of the love of money. It must be jarring, at least, to be treated as a walking cash point and not a person with spiritual and emotional needs by those who should care about the latter. How must the wealthy be manipulated at times, to give constantly, through creative misuse of the Bible? The question of whether they are really loved and appreciated may well haunt people who are wined and dined by those who eventually will seek a donation for something or other. This can be true, even while it might be intoxicating to have the kind of economic power that makes people want to be around you because you have the money and connections to make things happen. But here we find that the leaders of SPAC Nation, who exhibited great wealth, preyed upon young people who had none. Taking advantage of their aspirations for social mobility, these young people were forced to labour for the success of an institution they had no control over. Their sacrifices – sometimes life-changing in terms of levels of debt which would impact their financial futures – were demanded in the name of God, but for the benefit of those in charge.

If the love of almightiness or omnipotence leads us to idolatry – in that it confuses whatever seems successful in numerical terms with the divine – then we must learn to distinguish between ideas of success that stand in contradiction to the objectives of the way of Jesus and those that are consistent. We must resist the sometimes capitalistic or imperialistic models of Christian ministry which tell us expansion into spaces occupied by others is the core way the gospel should be shared. By this I do not mean to say that we do not want to see love, justice, peace and righteousness increase – of course we want more people to experience goodness and joy. But we should accept that we are not the only ones who might bring it. Even within the Church we often disagree about what 'good news' consists of. We all have blind spots which mean we cannot trust ourselves to have a full enough picture of what is needed. We cannot have confidence that our view of God, the Bible or ethical questions is the correct and complete one, without the need to confer with our wider family within the faith and beyond. It is important that we admit to ourselves that our judgement can be inadequate even with the best of intentions. We might be motivated by more than a simple desire to see people grow in their own journeys of faith. We probably have strong ideas about what it means to grow in faith, which are usually impacted by the way we have experienced it, or the way we think it should be. And when we have power, we are more at risk of using it to coerce people in the way we think they should go.

A story that helps us to think about power, economics and resisting almightiness can be found in the story of the widow's mite. The short story is recalled in Mark 12.41–44 and Luke 21.1–4 and it begins with Jesus sitting down in the temple watching as people give their offerings into the treasury. The version in Mark reads:

> Many rich people threw in large amounts. But a poor widow came and put in two very small copper coins, worth only a few cents. Calling his disciples to him, Jesus said, 'Truly I tell you, this poor widow has put more into the treasury than all the others. They all gave out of their wealth; but she, out of her poverty, put in everything – all she had to live on.'

This is not, I believe, a story that should encourage us to give without due consideration of our needs. However, this is precisely the kind of Scripture that would be easily manipulated for that purpose. Jesus does not use this story to propel himself into a sermon or teaching about giving, so we should be wary about doing that ourselves, especially when it is in our interest to get people to give, since our motives will be tainted. Instead, Jesus makes an observation, or a judgement, comparing the giver who has a lot, and the giver who has a little. He uses this moment to correct the temptation to imagine that God is somehow more pleased by those who have lots of money and give lots to religious work. He is teaching his disciples to see generosity differently. Across many of our cultures, the financially rich are treated differently from those who are materially poor. We collectively have made it so that the rich get better education, safer homes, better health care and food, better quality clothes and access to leisure and creative activities. We can even do this in our churches, to our shame. We have ways of letting members or 'partners' with money dominate what is preached, which projects are launched and cancelled, who gets jobs or is denied a job, and even what food is served (as I have experienced). We provide special meals, experiences and access for the wealthy, while looking past those who do not have enough money to make them important in our eyes.

What strikes me about this story is that Jesus does not condemn the widow for giving a little. He does not introduce shame into the narrative by watching this woman and asking why she didn't give more. He does not respond by saying 'Giving is a sign of our love for God; see how little she loves God! How much will the work of God be advanced by her measly coins?!' Her offering was not compared to the rich in a way that would problematize her. Jesus does not even launch into a socio-economic analysis of why she only has pennies while others have so much. This would be my gut instinct, to be honest, and I have concern for her, if it was true that she had given all she had to the temple. I remember being in a church meeting when a pastor used the Scripture to manipulate people to give money, promising them a return, and seeing a woman who was visibly not rich searching around in her bag for coins. I was angry at the thought of her 'giving all she had' under the coercion of a man in a fancy suit. But we know that, as a Jew, Jesus was raised to be concerned for widows, as the

Jewish law included many laws to protect them. And we know he had no problem calling out the religious authorities when he needed to. But here, Jesus focuses on this woman's actions as worthy of praise. Jesus extended trust in her and believed she had given her best, and that is all he had to say about her.

What does this have to teach us then, in a world of almightiness, global capitalism and financial abuse in the Church? We are invited here to reimagine our economic world otherwise. If, in God's economy, the intention rather than the final number has significance, then we are challenged to value the seemingly small because of its huge spiritual significance. The young intern – who should be paid a living wage, by the way – gives of their time and expertise, and this must be valued as the best they have to give. They should not be considered unimportant or less valuable than the donor who can write the cheques that help pay the intern's salary. The parent with a young family who can attend one service and maybe leaves midway through should not be treated as undedicated or compared unfavourably to the person who can commit to being on several teams. We have to trust that each is giving their best. The person who stops attending or giving in any way, as they deal with the pressures of life, but who prays at home, should not be judged as faithless – they are giving all they have. The small congregation with limited means, but faithful in prayer and love for God and the community, is to be treasured in a world that does not understand the wisdom of the pearl of great price.[21] This story is a plea for mercy, for challenging our assumptions and our preference for the wealthy in money or other ways.

It is also a lesson in respecting people's right under God, to decide for themselves what they can afford, and to set boundaries even in relation to those things deemed good and holy. I will deal with boundaries in detail in Chapter 6, but here I only want to note that in the case of the rich and the poor widow, there is no one twisting Scripture to get them to give. If there had been, this story would, I am sure, have gone very differently, and similar maybe to the turning over of the tables.

The widow gave out of the abundance of her faith and love, out of the richness of her spiritual stores, even while in monetary terms it seemed tiny. The offering that moved Jesus was the one others would have mocked as insignificant and useless.

Conclusion

I hope this chapter enables us to better understand how our theological imagination – here I mean the ideas we have about God as almighty – can betray us when it comes to how we think about ourselves, those who lead, and those who follow them or us. These assumptions about God's power can, without us always knowing, lead us to dangerous conclusions about what it means to serve God, and to lead others. In pursuit of even wonderful ends, we can resort to tactics that do harm to others, because our eyes are fixed on the vision we are striving for without us reflecting on the cost of getting there. The determination to grow and expand by any means necessary inevitably ends in exploitation and destruction, with people made in God's own image ending up as collateral damage. And it is also true that there are those, as in the case of SPAC Nation, who deliberately seek out the vulnerable, to devour them, for their own ends. In the widow's mite, we find a model of spiritual economics that values the small and good over the large and 'impressive', which should – if we hope to – enable us to safeguard ourselves and others from the exploitation of those whose gods are might and mammon.

Notes

1 See, as an example, Thomas Aquinas, *The Power of God*, trans. Richard J. Regan (Oxford: Oxford University Press, 2012), pp. 19–20.

2 In this case I consider the masculine pronoun to be appropriate since this way of thinking about divine power tends to be modelled on patriarchal dominance.

3 Karl Barth, *Dogmatics in Outline* (London: SCM Press, 1949), p. 48.

4 Barth, *Dogmatics in Outline*, p. 48.

5 1 Corinthians 12.4–8: 'There are diversities of gifts, but the same Spirit. There are differences of ministries, but the same Lord. And there are diversities of activities, but it is the same God who works all in all. But the manifestation of the Spirit is given to each one for the profit of all: for to one is given the word of wisdom through the Spirit, to another the word of knowledge through the same Spirit' (NKJV).

6 Katelyn Beaty, *Celebrities for Jesus: How Personas, Platforms and Profits are Hurting the Church* (Grand Rapids, MI: Brazos Press, 2022), pp. 71–2.

7 Noel Phillips, 'The Church where Drugs and Knives are Left at the Altar', *BBC News*, 1 February 2018, https://www.bbc.co.uk/news/uk-42887653 (accessed 3.07.2024).

8 The Charity Commission, 'Charity Regulator Opens Inquiry into SPAC Nation', 13 December 2019, https://www.gov.uk/government/news/charity-regulator-opens-inquiry-into-spac-nation (accessed 4.07.2024).

9 Nadine White and Emma Youle, 'SPAC Nation: Allegations of Safeguarding Abuses in "Trap Houses" Linked to Controversial Church', *Huffpost*, 9 November 2019, https://www.huffingtonpost.co.uk/entry/spac-nation-scandal-safeguarding_uk_5dc5a907e4b00927b2329c3c (accessed 3.07.2024); Nadine White and Emma Youle, 'SPAC Nation: Rogue Pastors Accused of Pressuring Youth to Donate Blood for Money for Church Funds', *Huffpost*, 11 December 2019, https://www.huffingtonpost.co.uk/entry/spac-nation-sell-blood-for-money_uk_5def9bb8e4b07f6835b958f5 (accessed 3.07.2024); Nadine White and Emma Youle, 'SPAC Nation: What we Know about Church whose Members are Accused of Fraud and Abuse', *Huffpost*, 16 December 2019, https://www.huffingtonpost.co.uk/entry/spac-nation-fraud-abuse-panorama_uk_5df6e471e4b03aed50f0650b (accessed 3.07.2024).

10 White and Youle, 'SPAC Nation: Allegations'.

11 BBC, *Catch Her if You Can*, BBC, https://www.bbc.co.uk/programmes/p08vwr8y, first broadcast 3 November 2020.

12 Vic Santoro, Instagram, @VicSantoro.

13 BBC Panorama, 'Conned by my Church', *BBC*, https://www.bbc.co.uk/programmes/mooocfr5, first broadcast 16 December 2019.

14 BBC News, 'SPAC Nation: No Criminal Probe into Evangelical Church', *BBC News*, 11 February 2020, https://www.bbc.co.uk/news/uk-england-london-51459741 (accessed 4.07.2024).

15 BBC News, 'SPAC Nation: London Church Wound up over Financial Mismanagement', *BBC News*, 17 June 2022, https://www.bbc.co.uk/news/uk-england-london-61844094 (accessed 3.07.2024).

16 House of Commons, UK Parliament, HC Deb (Wednesday 8 January 2020), Vol. 669, https://hansard.parliament.uk/Commons/2020-01-08/debates/04DE1B71-C7FD-46EE-BDC5-B11182AD9BF5/SPACNation (accessed 4.07.2024).

17 House of Commons, HC Deb (Wednesday 8 January 2020).

18 House of Commons, HC Deb (Wednesday 8 January 2020).

19 On 4 December several news outlets reported 'pastor' Tobi had lost his appeal to remain in the UK and will be deported to Nigeria facing fraud allegations. His attempts to paint himself as a community leader, lauded by politicians, failed to convince the Home Office and his immigration hearing. Inside Croydon, 'Founder of "Church of Bling" to be Deported as Illegal Immigrant', *Inside Croydon*, https://insidecroydon.com/2024/12/04/founder-of-church-of-bling-to-be-deported-as-illegal-immigrant/ (accessed 5.12.2024).

20 Lisa Oakley and Justin Humphreys, *Escaping the Maze of Spiritual Abuse: Creating Healthy Christian Cultures* (London: SPCK, 2019), p. 54.

21 Matthew 13.45–46: 'Again, the kingdom of heaven is like a merchant looking for fine pearls. When he found one of great value, he went away and sold everything he had and bought it.'

4

On Principalities and Powers

When it comes to conversations about problematic values or behaviour, we (Christians) can speak, at times, as if there is a hard dividing line between the Church and 'the world'. We talk boldly as if there is some inherent goodness about claiming to be Christian or belonging to a church. We imagine it is obvious who is Christian and who is not, and where the wisdom is, and where it is not. We can react with surprise, then, when it turns out people are not rushing to hear what we think, nor giving us privileges in public conversations. Can they not see the wisdom or important moral guidance we have to offer?

This binary way of thinking about reality, as is the case with all categorization processes, helps our brain make sense of the world more easily. Prejudices and other forms of black-and-white thinking reduce the level of work our brain has to do, by making quick connections. The problem is, they prevent us from doing the necessary critical reflection. So rather than thinking about where we might see God, or indeed the presence of evil, on a case-by-case basis, we can take a short cut and presume something is either good or evil based on speedy meaning making. The problem is that we do need to consider certain questions with more nuance than assumptions will allow. Let's take our reflection on the Church for example. The hard dividing line, designed theologically to reduce complexity, encourages us to see the gathered church in the building as holy, safe and trustworthy. We focus on passages that call us 'holy', 'set free from sin' and 'the family of God' and this reinforces the assumption that we are safe here. We seek to reinforce this ideal and avoid whatever (or whoever) disturbs this image. Our brains want to keep things simple. We let our guard down and encourage others to do the same (directly or indirectly) and we all become vulnerable without noticing it. We start to imagine, because of the impact of our theology or the theologies we hear, that we are safer than we actually are. This inadvertently leads to us having what we might call 'an over-realized theology of sanctification' regarding the Church. In other words, we start to believe we Christians are better than we really are. We imagine there is less danger of scammers, predators, liars and thieves than we might find outside. And we fail to maintain the safeguards we usually use to protect ourselves when we are out and about in 'the world'.

If theologies cause us to be unwisely relaxed in the midst of Christian communities where dangers do lurk, then they simultaneously cause us to be hyper-vigilant regarding 'worldly' dangers. By this I do not mean that we should not be on guard for legitimate risks to our lives of faith. We must be able to discern when we are being tempted to worship idols like wealth, and to serve money instead of God, for example. This kind of reflection is essential to our discipleship. But we can get to the point of uncritically condemning what we perceive as happening in 'the culture' or coming from 'the world'. This can often be based on inaccurate assumptions or interpretations, when we haven't even taken time to understand what is really happening. 'The culture' and 'the world' become shorthand for anything that cannot be traced directly to a white Christian idea of orthodoxy and Christian living. So Black Lives Matter protests or any racial justice conversation is considered a 'worldly' distraction. And having gender-inclusive toilets in a public space is blown so far out of proportion it is assumed humanity itself is now under threat. We imagine that in the wider world, we as Christians are under threat and vulnerable so we need to have our guard up. We reject learning and lessons from 'the world' even when they are consistent with what many might describe as the values of the Christian faith. We reject wisdom that comes to us from anyone who does not profess Christian faith and we certainly do not imagine they can teach us anything about God.

But I have been around long enough to see through these strict binaries. I grew up hearing 'principalities and powers' described as demonic and destructive spiritual forces. They could be defeated, we believed, through prayer and sometimes fasting. They might be connected to secular institutions or cultural shifts which were believed to be incompatible or even hostile to the Church. But what happens when the principalities come in the forms of cathedrals, church systems and boards full of Christians? What do you do when 'the powers' have the title 'Bishop' or 'Pastor' and wear a cassock or robe? In this chapter I seek to complicate the simple lines we draw in our thinking about good and bad powers, sacred and secular space, and the places from which we might need deliverance.

Jesus and which powers?

The latest intervention on the themes of power in the Bible and Christian living is entitled *Jesus and the Powers* and written by N. T. Wright and Michael F. Bird. In this book they hope to address some of the pressing questions facing churches in the West. In defining 'powers' they turn to Paul, whose writings offer often vague and inconclusive definitions and uses of the word. The conclusion is that for Paul 'the powers' are 'both (what we would call) "earthly" and (what we would call) "heavenly" or "supernatural".'[1] This should not suggest to us that Paul is discussing two distinct sets of 'power', some earthly and some heavenly, but that 'the powers' are indeed both spiritual and tangible.

Wright and Bird highlight an essential theological and moral theme, that of the Church's relationship to empires 'biblical and burgeoning',[2] as well as what are for them important matters for Christians to understand:

> how to build for the kingdom in our cities and suburbs ... the time for obedience to the State and the time for disobedience to the State ... where the church sits between principalities and powers ... how we can pursue human flourishing, how we might work for the common good, and how we can pursue the things that make for peace in a time of political turmoil such as has not been seen since the 1930s.[3]

These are, as I have said, essential questions, which the book goes on to explore through a combination of public and political theologies, biblical studies and theological ethics. And yet the book falls into the trap, I think, of presuming there is a hard line between those who belong to the Church (in this case churches in the West, especially the UK and at times the USA) and those who belong to 'the world'. Whether or not it is meant to be read as a conflict between 'them' and 'us', this is how the language of 'Church' and 'powers' or 'world' sounds – these are made up of people after all. There is a recognition throughout the book of the European churches' complicity in the Crusades, in colonial violence and the transatlantic slave trade as examples. But rather than being considered an ongoing pattern of behaviour, these events are discussed as mere blips on the Church's historical record that should not cause us to stop and rethink any of our claims regarding the Church or those of us called 'Christians'. We should, no matter how bad things have got, or how bad things are, continue to speak well of churches and put our hope in them (that is, in ourselves – since they are writing as and to Christians) as the source from which a better future might emerge.

My critique is not that the Western Church and its theologians should seek to be perfect before engaging in any public or political theologizing or engagement. However, I do think there must be a recognition of the deep-seated historic distortions inherent in some aspects of its theology in the past and in the present. Today, theology can (despite even the best intentions) reiterate certain of these errors. This includes when attempting to name the Church's 'missional vocation' or 'kingdom witness'[4] in relation to the powers. Thankfully, Western Christianity and its theologians are not representative of the whole global Church. Recognizing the limits of white Western appraisals of 'the powers' opens up space for even greater critical reflection.

While some European Christians were colluding with 'the powers' by trading slaves, running chapels above slave-holding cells and setting up theological colleges on plantations, the African Christians who had been enslaved were resisting them. Through critical reading and preaching of the biblical text, theologizing in radical ways, they held ground, in the face of the 'Christian' powers that sought to dehumanize and oppress them. There is an absence of such a notion of Christian 'worldliness' or indeed the resistance to 'Christian' powers in the entirety of the book in question. I am reminded as I reflect on this of a recent book by pastor, scholar and activist Revd Otis Moss III entitled *Dancing in the Darkness*. In it, he describes the fear he and his congregation felt when members of the fundamentalist Westboro Baptist 'church' from Kansas, USA, arrived on their doorstep. Branded by some watchdog organizations as a hate group due to their violently homophobic and racist slogans and protest materials, they consider themselves true and faithful believers. They arrived at Trinity United Church of Christ (TUCC) in Chicago around the time it was revealed that the then-senator Barack Obama had attended while Moss's predecessor Jeremiah Wright was senior pastor. Moss writes:

> Some of the Westboro people carried signs with outrageous claims about abortion and our church, while others shouted racist epithets through megaphones. Mothers and grandmothers had to move through this gauntlet of provocation

and hate while trying to shield their little ones. Our spiritual home was under assault.⁵

In response Moss sought to lead his congregation to draw on their Black spiritual heritage, a heritage in which Africans deconstructed and reconstructed ideas about Christianity which were too often dominated by white supremacist ideals and economic interests. The choir surrounded the protesters with singing and clapping, with the deacons then asking the protesters to join them in prayer, which they refused to do. The TUCC congregation prayed in what Moss calls 'Pentecostal' form, so much so that 'the atmosphere changed' and the protesters were eventually overcome and left.

This was a meeting of two sets of people who both claimed the title Christian and faith in the person Jesus (though their faiths and their concepts of Jesus are noticeably incompatible with each other). This is the kind of conflict, as opposed to that of the Church or kingdom of God and the world, that should also occupy our minds today. For some, this may be considered a distraction from the matters of evangelism and witness to the wider world. In which case, we must ignore such concerns and return to what Wright and Bird are commending to us. But what if the battle for what it means to be Christian is core to the political theologies being presented? What if these fundamental disagreements within the Church impact on and undermine any political or public ambitions for power and influence that Christians may have?

In their book, Wright and Bird have not sought to think critically about power among Christians or within the Church or churches, and so it might be unfair to offer these critiques. But since they do recognize the Church's tendency to act in complicity with the powers rather than resist them, I feel it is fair to push their analysis further and deeper in several important places. As I have already claimed in my introduction to this chapter, it seems clear to me, in the biblical text, in the history of the Church and in our lived experiences of churches, that there is much more going on than a simple conflict between Jesus (or Christians) and political authorities or 'powers'. Reading Wright and Bird's account of Jesus' trial and crucifixion, or in their account of the powers the Church must resist, I wondered what it might mean to recognize or name religious powers among these. It is indeed true that Jesus is brought before Pilate – who we might think of as a secular authority – but he ends up there because of plotting by the religious powers of his day. In their bid to gain control over the people and to stamp out his claims and his embodiment of God's loving reign, they plot consistently to kill him. It is because of *them* that he ends up before Pilate who himself has to admit, 'I see no fault in him.' Jesus is not simply living a life in conflict with political powers, but with principalities upheld and even created by religious believers who consider themselves to be the faithful.

The same issue plays out, I think, in Wright and Bird's reading of what resistance means for churches in the West today. They name several areas for the Church to stand and resist: against totalitarianism, Christian nationalism, civic totalism and resurgent empires.[6] Without getting drawn into the details of these categories, safe to say there is nothing I would disagree with in these suggestions. What is missing – and again, this is not the stated aim of the book but it does matter to my mind – is the naming of the kinds of religious and theological powers that the Church must discern and resist. It is so much easier to focus on the dust in the eye of 'the world' than the plank in the eyes of the Church. Some of the most pressing power problems faced by Christians and churches today are not caused primarily by external authorities, but those which are internal. They are initiated by individuals and groups past and present, embedded in systems, structures, histories and perspectives that undermine the work of the Spirit and the life of God's people. We need to be able to recognize what we might think of as evil principalities and powers, within the Church.

To do this, I will think about the kingdom which, I agree

with the authors, is what we as Christians are here to pray for, welcome within and among us, and participate in. We find a curious parable in the Gospels, which I expect might rescue us from delusions about the Church, and any unwise desire to put all our hope in it, as opposed to putting our hope in God, the source of all power, the work of Christ and the Spirit who remains with us as an advocate.

What's in our field?

In Matthew 13.24–30, we find the following parable which complicates our dualisms regarding the Church and the kingdom, and 'the world'. It reads:

> Another parable He put forth to them, saying: 'The kingdom of heaven is like a man who sowed good seed in his field; but while men slept, his enemy came and sowed tares among the wheat and went his way. But when the grain had sprouted and produced a crop, then the tares also appeared. So the servants of the owner came and said to him, "Sir, did you not sow good seed in your field? How then does it have tares?" He said to them, "An enemy has done this." The servants said to him, "Do you want us then to go and gather them up?" But he said, "No, lest while you gather up the tares you also uproot the wheat with them. Let both grow together until the harvest, and at the time of harvest I will say to the reapers, 'First gather together the tares and bind them in bundles to burn them, but gather the wheat into my barn.'"'

We will leave the last section about the burning bundles for someone else's book. The point I want to make here is that in this parable, the kingdom is compared to a space in which there are multiple kinds of seed sown, and these seeds then produce crops. It is not immediately obvious that tares have been sown among the wheat; wheat and tares don't even look different initially. There is no neat line between the wheat and the tares, otherwise it would be easy to uproot what was destructive and nurture what would produce food. Instead, the tares will be watered along with the wheat, they will benefit from the same sunshine and all have the same opportunities to grow. It is only at the point that the grain sprouts that we can tell what is and is not wheat. And then the reaper can separate out what is good for food, and what is useless.

When the disciples ask Jesus to explain this parable, he tells them:

> 'The one who sowed the good seed is the Son of Man. The field is the world, and the good seed stands for the people of the kingdom. The weeds are the people of the evil one, and the enemy who sows them is the devil. The harvest is the end of the age, and the harvesters are angels.'

He goes on to say that, 'At the end of the age, the Son of Man will send out his angels, and they will weed out of his kingdom everything that causes sin and all who do evil.' This explanation is (I am sorry to say, Jesus) quite unclear. First, we read 'the field is the world'; then it seems to switch to the field being 'the kingdom', from which angels must weed out evil. First, the explanation tells us that the seeds are people – either people of the kingdom or people of the evil one. Then we read that the evil is broader: 'everything that causes sin *and* all who do evil'. So we find ourselves in a bit of an interpretive conundrum.

Wherever we might land – and I am no biblical scholar – the overarching sense we get is that trying to draw a straight line between the good people and the bad, the world and the kingdom, or the world and the Church is not straightforward. More than this, it might even be considered a fool's errand. There are some obvious lines one might draw of course, where evil is obvious because of the undeniable harm done to God's creation. We would not want to think these could somehow be compatible with the kingdom of God. There is throughout the Gospels, and in Jesus' own words, a sense that being a Christian looks very different from not being one. But I wonder whether this field with mixed seeds is a more realistic account of what we can actually expect: that there is much grey and we cannot always discern the difference. We should be less confident about the lines we draw, even if we are standing in the field or one of the plants themselves, right up close to the ground.

When we read a parable like this, we can be met with the urge to find meaning for our contemporary moment. This is of course why many of us read the Bible. But in a passage like this, that sets up a binary, we need to be mindful of our blind spots. This is core to handling the power of the Scriptures and our interpretation. We might, when reading this, be quick to label ourselves as the 'wheat' in the metaphor – but how do we know who we really are? To what extent can we truly judge ourselves correctly? We might judge others as 'tares' due to our limited understanding, and see it is justice for them to be burned, metaphorically speaking. But maybe we are the ones choking life out of others, like a weed, despite our best intentions.

The parable for me is an important reminder that as we hope to welcome and participate in the kingdom of God, we are in the company of some who, if they had their way, might hold us back from the fullness of life we hope for. This is the nature of 'tares'. We are all at risk of functioning in this way from time to time, but some have committed to this destructive path. They may imagine themselves to be wheat; after all, wheat and tares look similar. But when the fullness of who they are emerges, they leave nothing with which others can be nurtured. They have only consumed nutrients and life from others, for their own advancement, while offering nothing in exchange.

While we might read such a description and think of individuals who might fit with it, it is the case that religious systems and organizations, even structures, can function in this way. They can be like weeds in a field, in which people ask: how did we end up here, we only sowed good seed, didn't we? Well, yes, but an enemy found their way in – he might even have been let in through deliberate fault – and now the field is full of weeds growing among the wheat.

This should humble those of us who imagine that the field in which we are planted can only ever be good, sustaining and nurturing. While this is a parable about the kingdom, enough time spent in churches will surely convince us the same could be said of congregations and church life. We do not always know what we are or what we are becoming, but in the fullness of the season, so much can be revealed. It is this awareness of what can lie in the fields we inhabit that enables us to be more vigilant about the dangers that lurk in spaces we consider sacred. And it is this healthy awareness, that the lines are not as straightforward as we would like, that adds nuance to our reading of the division between the Church and the 'world'.

All analogies have their limits though, and I do not read this parable as suggesting that those things or people who might function as weeds have no chance to be changed. We are *not* wheat or weeds, but human beings in the hands of a gracious God. We have the capacity for consciousness of ourselves and others, our choices and actions and their effects. The overarching story of the gospel is one in which repentance is possible, as the Spirit makes us aware of where we are falling short and brings about the possibilities for goodness, love and righteousness which remain available even if we turn out to behave as weeds.

Unity: Power narratives

The Bible is full of messages about the importance and beauty of a people who are united. We are reminded that we are all individual parts of one united body, and that it is beautiful when we dwell together in unity.[7] Jesus prayed for unity among his disciples in John 17, so we know it matters. But it seems to me that there is a difference between a genuine togetherness graced by the Spirit and a false unity brought about by coercion and force. Attempting to rush towards unity without undertaking the diligent work of listening, confession, repentance and reparation can only ever produce the latter. But sadly, this is what we tend to be occupied with. The rush to a false unity is helped along by the politeness we know all too well as part of English culture. But this gets in the way of actual Christian unity, which requires confrontation and much of what we would call 'awkwardness'.

Though this might be controversial for some, I am convinced that we cannot create unity. Some will, of course, consider me a bad Christian for confessing such a thing: 'What about the prayer of our Lord Jesus, that we would all be one?' Well, I say that the point is that it was a prayer, something Jesus was asking God to enact. That means, first, that unity was not a reality even right at the start of the Church's life when things were much simpler in many ways. And second, Jesus seems to have understood that simply telling them to be united would not make it so. This would literally take divine intervention. There are all kinds of ways we can create a sense of unity, and I do not mean to say that nothing good can come from attempting to bring people together. But the desire to be together – not just together with people who look or think like us but the whole body of believers – is not something you can teach or train into someone. This desire is a love born of the Spirit, as we encounter and learn from those who are different from us.

We are a body, whether we like it or not, and this means that in some mysterious way, through the Spirit, we who confess faith in Jesus are one. We who in our words and actions, and intentions, invite the Spirit continually to fill our lives, and submit to her leading, are unified in ways that remain true, even if we cannot always embody or exemplify them in our real lives. And the truth is that while we are one, we do not often recognize or respond to this. But this is not surprising. Some of us are not even at one with ourselves. We do not know what it is to accept ourselves and be at peace with who we really are, with God. We are in denial about our desires, habits and personalities, shrouded in shame, presenting a false acceptable version to those around us. How, when we are not reconciled within ourselves, would we even go about attempting to create that oneness with others? We would only be unifying a false self with others. The Spirit's work of reconciliation, of creating unity, is what we need to submit to. In this way, we can be sure that unity will be genuine. It will not be cheap for us but expensive for others. It will require us to face ourselves as we are and to tell the truth. We will be convicted regarding our own failings in this regard, and come to understand the costliness of the unity we say we want. We do not get to decide the price for our neighbour, especially when we are in a position of relative privilege when compared to them – this is the very way to miss the point. We do not get to set terms for what 'they' (who we look down upon, if we are honest with ourselves) must do to be united with 'us'. The Christian question, the reflection we are invited to by the one who called us to love not judge our neighbour, is 'What do I need to do to be reconciled with you, especially the you I have sinned against?'

Our hope for unity is a beautiful thing, but our urgency can lead to dishonesty. Unity cannot exist where patterns of injustice remain intact. It is important to recognize that when unity is being valorized as a Christian virtue, there is often little attention being paid to the differences in power that shape those relationships. Our relationships are rarely (if ever) equal, whether between diverse individuals or groups. So when we demand unity or value unity, what do we mean? Unity too often means the minority or less powerful must be silent so the dominating person or group can carry on as usual without the disturbance brought about when we hear 'other' perspectives. Unity can mean that a person or group of people must give up their hopes and dreams and accept whatever crumbs they are given by those who have more money, power or resources. Unity can require that we play a role in false friendships and shallow transactional connections, not calling out hypocrisy or lack of integrity. It can mean pretending to listen with genuine openness, while you are secretly gaining what you need to launch your next assault.

Unity for many of us has meant being silenced so things can remain as they are, or go back to how they were. When you are not allowed to ask genuine questions or disagree because you will 'threaten unity', the message becomes misused to exert control. In many stories of spiritual abuse, unity is used to censor, control or coerce people.[8] Where unity is preached as a response to the cries of those who speak up about their suffering, their pain and exclusion, we can be sure it is being weaponized to support the powerful. When 'unity' is used to distract us from listening to the still small voices in our communities, we can be sure it is being abused to maintain the status quo. We are invited instead to scratch below the surface of what is being said to ask: who will maintain power and who will lose it, in the unity that is being demanded? The price for unity can be far too high, and borne almost exclusively by those who are already forced to carry burdens too heavy for them. Those who are in positions of power too often benefit from the unity they gain by manipulation, without having to address their own wrongdoing. The demand for unity (some use the language of reconciliation) without repentance on the part of the wrongdoer is like asking me to share a meal with someone whom I have just caught lacing my food with poison. You will have to excuse me if I suddenly lose my appetite.

Complete unhindered relational unity, in which we are happy to be part of this body, within which we share one desire, one love, one hope, may be far beyond what we can aspire to in this life. Part of what it means to have eschatological hope is that we know that what we hope for – and what Jesus hoped for – will not be accomplished until the Last Day. At the end of time, once all this is said and done and there is no more agreeing or disagreeing, then this unity will be fulfilled. As we are united as beings before our creator, no longer 'seeing through a mirror dimly', then it will all be clear and we will be united in this clarity. Until then, it seems, we are all looking through squinted eyes and seeing very different shapes and visions. We are united, ultimately, in our inability to see God, ourselves or the world as they/we fully are. We are one in our need for correctors to our vision and our need for God to continue to remove the scales from our eyes.

Of course, I have presumed so far that we are talking about unity between those who might disagree but continue to prioritize walking 'in the spirit' of Christ in their lives and ministries. I am assuming there is a deep openness to being taught by the rabbi from Nazareth, and led by the Spirit in ways that will transform our whole lives. But this is not always the case. In some instances, unity is demanded by and with those who, if they had their way, would prevent us from having basic goods needed for our thriving. Within the Church, historically and today, are those who would leave us to poverty, would deny us the right to family and cause us to be isolated and alone for our entire lives. There are those who would deny us space to fulfil our vocation and frustrate our sense of calling and our hopes. Others would deny us a place at the table of our Lord because we are judged by them to be unworthy.

What then does 'unity' mean in light of these stark realities? If it is not already clear, then I will say it as directly as I can – reconciliation and unity is impossible with those who do not love us. And sometimes this is what we are actually attempting in our churches – unity and reconciliation where there is no love. We may tolerate people who are in our churches with whom we disagree, but this is not love. We might listen to a person, while trying our best to find ways to undermine their argument, but this is not love. We might do our best to prevent them having access to some good thing, because we have decided they should not have it, for some good we have decided is better, but this is not love. We might delude ourselves into thinking that just because we have not actively harmed a person or group, or said something violent, that we are loving them, but this is not love. Love is to desire good for your neighbour, to the point of being actively involved in ensuring they receive it as fully as possible. It is wanting the best for them – not the best you have decided, but the best they have chosen – so much so that you will stand with them and push with them as they pursue it. It is wanting for them the same joys and pleasures you want for yourself, and without any of the pain or suffering you may have had. It is being willing to have difficult conversations when they will help the other get to that flourishing they hope for. It is giving what you can to help them thrive in the ways they hope to, and respecting their boundaries when they are not ready or do not want to receive. Love can only exist when we listen, for that is how we learn how to love our neighbour in the ways they need. The bonds of love deepen over time, as we show up and prove ourselves to be full of the love of God whose name we claim. From consistent love comes trust, and from trust, the willingness to be united as one.

The prayer of Jesus, then, is a prayer that depends on love, since we cannot be united without it. And in our disagreements and debates and infighting, love, pure and uncorrupted, is not what we find flowing in abundance. Love is a power, though, which we underestimate even as we think about principalities and powers, seen and unseen. It is because of love, in the end, that Jesus endures the Cross and shames the powers. These powers imagine that brutal violence can be used for a good cause, and might even be what God requires. 'Love is stronger than death', we read. And this is not simply interpersonal love, which we continue to enjoy on some level even when the lover or beloved has died. But it is true, I think, on a systemic level. Desire, and the alignment of desire with consistent action, has the power to create new worlds and even new churches. I am not thinking here about a fleeting sentiment, but a desire that is embedded in our core, our motivation, an unwavering, persistent determination to act.

I began this chapter by warning us not to be naive about the dangers that we find in places we are encouraged to see as safe, holy, even familial. And I end with the same plea. There are many loves shaping our churches and our lives, not all of them consistent with the way of God seen in Christ Jesus. And it is too easy, as we have seen in some of the cases of abuse discussed and to be discussed, for us to be deceived ourselves. We can think we love God and our neighbour, when in truth we despise the latter and thus the former. There can be no love of God whom we cannot see, if we do not love those we *can* see; this is the warning of John's letter (1 John 4.20). And so the thwarting of the powers, almighty as they seem, is not, contrary to pragmatic wisdom, in seeking to ascend to their heights. Whether within the Church or beyond, we can overcome principalities in the same way as Christ did: by letting love shine brightly enough to reveal the folly of hate, of self-righteousness and of dominating power. It is in the foolishness of love that the strong (and almighty), will be confounded. Amen.

Notes

1 N.T. Wright and Michael F. Bird, *Jesus and the Powers: Christian Political Witness in an Age of Totalitarian Terror and Dysfunctional Democracies* (London: SPCK, 2024), p. 51.
2 Wright and Bird, *Jesus and the Powers*, p. viii.
3 Wright and Bird, *Jesus and the Powers*, p. viii.
4 Wright and Bird, *Jesus and the Powers*, p. x.
5 Otis Moss III, *Dancing in the Darkness: Spiritual Lessons for Turbulent Times* (New York, NY: Simon and Schuster, 2023), pp. 98–9.
6 Wright and Bird, *Jesus and the Powers*, pp. 122–49.
7 1 Corinthians 12.12–27; Psalm 113.1.
8 Lisa Oakley and Justin Humphreys, *Escaping the Maze of Spiritual Abuse: Creating Healthy Christian Cultures* (London: SPCK, 2019), pp. 55–6.

5

Sanctifying Suffering: The Cross and Christian Abuse

Jesus' death is of central importance across Christian traditions. But the specific meaning we should draw from the torturous murder of Jesus is what makes the crucial difference. For those of us who belong or have belonged to the more Evangelical end of the Church, the Cross, we are sometimes taught, is what eternal life hinges on in a very particular way. 'For all have sinned and fallen short of God's glory', we commonly cite. We have incurred God's righteous judgement, and as in Jewish religious law, a sacrifice had to be made to atone for that sin. Rather than demanding never-ending sacrifices of sheep and goats, God has chosen to take this sacrifice on Godself, by becoming human in Jesus and laying down his life. Jesus has become that sacrifice that, once and for all, clears the slate between God and humanity. Because of Jesus' sacrifice, we are now able to enter into relationship with God when we, as individuals, recognize and believe this account, and trust that in Christ we are now made one with God. We are invited, as a sign of our faith, to lay our lives down as 'living sacrifices', choosing to live not according to our own will, but in line with the will of God in Christ.

For those who belong to or are at least familiar with other corners of the Church, the emphasis on Jesus' death as a necessary sacrifice to appease God's wrath (however just it might be) may seem unusual. Jesus' death and the Cross itself do not always loom as large in the imaginations of our Christian family beyond the Evangelical world. Jesus' death is recognized as but one element of a story in which God is incarnated, born of the Virgin Mary, and lives a life embodying justice, love and peace. Jesus matters for our salvation not only because he dies, but mainly because he is born and lives, and lives again even after sin and death have done their worst. He matters because he demonstrates what it means to live a full life, abundantly filled with the Spirit, always in tune with the will of the Father. And his death is an example of the kind of violence we as humans are capable of, even in the face of divine beauty. The victory over sin and death in this account is found in the Resurrection, *not* primarily in the Cross.

These varying accounts of the Cross and Jesus' death have their roots in the different perspectives held by the Church's first theologians and subsequent years of debates.[1] There was not a golden age when all Christian theologians and church leaders shared one view on how we should understand the Cross – there are many metaphors, analogies and ideas provided in the Bible which give us different viewpoints on this mystery. But what we can do, I think, is judge them, in part at least, by their ethical implications – the consequences for our lived experiences. It is my view that an emphasis on God's wrath demanding Jesus' sacrifice, suffering and torture too easily lays the groundwork for abuses of power in Christian families, churches and organizations. This is why I have shifted my own emphasis when I discuss the Cross in any context. This is not because I want to give the impression that we can expect to have a life free of suffering or sacrifices as Christians – these are standard aspects of our human experience regardless of our faith or lack of it. And as Christians we can be sure our faith will cost us something, or at least it should, if we are following in the way of Jesus Christ. However, we need to ask hard questions about who exactly is having the say over what we are required to sacrifice or how we must suffer.

It is one thing to gain hope by choosing to see your own suffering as linked to the suffering of Christ. Or to teach

Christians that following Jesus faithfully will result in a desire to lay aside whatever hinders that journey. This has always been the truth of what it is to be Christian, but this does not have to lead to abuse. People can still be taught to discern for themselves what those sacrifices should be, or where enduring suffering will lead to perseverance, character and hope. It is a totally different thing to be coerced into a sacrifice because of fear or shame, and to be harmed and violated in ways that deny your agency, and refuse your right to have your say over your own life. This critique has long been laid out by Black, womanist and feminist theologians, as we so often speak from contexts where we have seen patterns of abuse spiritually legitimized using the language of 'necessary sacrifice'.

For some this will seem to go too far – there are many staunch defenders of what is called 'penal substitutionary atonement theory' and its relations. And those who would reject this understanding of the Cross can still idealize suffering. Even if we do not imagine Jesus was born to be a sacrifice for our sins, there is still the whole idea that his suffering was necessary to prove God's love or to win victory over the powers of sin and death. My plea is that all of us wrestle with the pastoral responsibility we have towards those we preach to and teach. Somewhere in your congregation – as I found recently – will be a woman who has survived or is surviving domestic violence and is theologizing through her suffering. Or there may be someone being overworked and underpaid in a Christian organization whose mental health is suffering, who imagines that this might be exactly what God wants for them, 'a cross they have to bear'. What does it mean to bear these stories in mind, even as we preach what we believe is true to the biblical accounts? How can you ensure people do not walk away imagining they must suffer abuse to please God?

In the stories we read about abuses of power in churches and Christian communities, the theme of suffering as good and necessary arises repeatedly. We cannot, if we want to root out abuse, leave untouched the narratives that allow it to happen.

This may not mean jettisoning one's entire atonement theory – though it might – but it means at least reckoning with how we might be inadvertently preparing people to accept abuse. This, of course, includes ourselves. I am under no illusion that those who abuse people with the help of theology have often also been spiritually abused in similar ways and often treat themselves with the same disdain that they act out on others. By this I do not mean they abuse themselves in precisely the same ways, but that they condemn themselves to suffering and torture, even as they do the same to others.

To explore these themes, we will examine the case of John Smyth and his physical abuse of schoolboys at an elite school in the UK as well as at a camp in Zimbabwe. With the help of womanist theologians Delores Williams and JoAnne Marie Terrell, we will consider the impact of believing there is 'power in the blood'.

Wounded for their transgressions? The case of John Smyth

John Smyth was a Christian barrister, licensed preacher and lay reader in the Church of England. He was deeply involved in the Iwerne (pronounced 'yew-un') Trust, a powerful conservative Evangelical organization of which he eventually became a trustee. The organization was founded to bring Evangelicalism to the heart of the British establishment, and as part of this it ran camps for upper-middle-class boys from elite public schools. Smyth is now known to have used his connections with Winchester College (the oldest public school in Britain) and the Iwerne camps to groom boys for abuse. He would often bring boys back to his home where he would take them to a purpose-built soundproof shed for beatings. Survivors reported that from the late 1970s, he would physically abuse them, stripping them and beating them until they bled.[2] In the early 1980s, the trustees advised him to leave the UK because survivors were coming forward. They did not report him to the police. He left for Zimbabwe in 1984, where his abuse of boys continued at the new camp he founded called Zambesi Holidays. Channel 4 aired two films about his abuse in 2017 which prompted a police investigation.[3] Smyth's abuse led to one known case of attempted suicide, and for others physical but also mental, emotional and psychological scars. In Zimbabwe, he was charged with the death of Guide Nyachuru, a boy found naked, bruised and dead the morning after he arrived at Smyth's camp in 1992.[4]

Many of the stories recalled in the Channel 4 report, and in the longest comprehensive account written by Andrew Graystone in *Bleeding for Jesus: John Smyth and the Cult of the Iwerne Camps*, demonstrate the way the Bible and theology were used to justify abuse.[5] But before we look at Smyth's particular actions, it is important to note how the culture of the Iwerne camps helped set the scene by promoting a particular kind of theological emphasis along with a determination to form a specific sort of masculinity. The boys were expected to submit to a strict programme and close monitoring by camp leaders. They disciplined their bodies through regular exercise, ice baths and rituals of punishment as well as spiritual activities like fasting and regular Bible studies. At the Iwerne camps, survivors recall the themes of Bible studies in the evening:

> The first evening would start with an introductory talk called something like 'who is Christ?' The next day would focus on sin, the fallenness of human beings, and their need for salvation. The third day was always about the death of Christ on the cross, and the need for individuals to respond in repentance.[6]

In the testimonies of survivors, they often speak of a sense of abandonment and emotional vulnerability due to being away at boarding school and detached from familial ties. This kind of theological messaging increased the sense of needing someone to lead them towards salvation. Left without their biological parents, Smyth positioned himself as the spiritual father and guide they needed to grow in faith and prove themselves worthy of God's love. He often directly quoted passages about sons and fathers, or parents and children, such as 2 Samuel 7.14, Hebrews 12.4–11 and Proverbs 13.24, to justify the abuse.[7]

But it is a particular theology of suffering, supported by a focus on the Cross and atonement, that is most profoundly implicated in the testimonies of survivors. In reports by survivors, we see how Christian theologies of suffering were used to justify the abuse. Smyth would tell Mark Stibbe, who went on to tell his story, 'You have to shed blood if you're really serious about dealing with sin', citing Hebrews 12.4: 'In your struggle against sin, you have not yet resisted to the point of shedding your blood.'[8] Beatings were given initially as a punishment for 'sins' they were made to write down and share with Smyth. However, eventually, the beatings were then used as a test of how far they were willing to go to show their faith. Smyth would tell his victims that they needed to demonstrate true repentance by allowing him to beat them. They needed to 'bleed for Jesus' and prove their loyalty and endurance; chillingly, he told them: 'The Lord's looking for more.' On hearing the accounts of survivors, Graystone has explained that, 'It was as much the shame of giving up on Jesus as the shame of revealing one's own vulnerability that made men keep coming back to Winchester for more lashes.'[9] Some of the boys at Winchester College were beaten over the course of three years, with some receiving thousands of lashes, often over 100 in a session. It was all kept hidden.

When reports such as these come to the surface, it is easy for us to see them as an extreme case or an exception to the rule. We then imagine that this kind of abuse, at least in terms of the beatings, is rare – which hopefully it is. But when we think of it as rare, we then imagine that the individual is the issue and they alone are to blame. Since we do not have dozens of cases like this – at least in public view – then we assume that we do not need to ask deeper questions about the theological perspectives underpinning such violations. Smyth was simply a bad apple on an otherwise good tree. His theology was sound, even if his actions were questionable. I do not mean to blame theology here, or a particular theory of atonement, in a very simplistic way. There are of course many people and leaders who will share an understanding of suffering and sacrifice as part of the Christian life, and would never imagine weaponizing those beliefs in this manner. But it is important to ask what was happening in Smyth's theological imagination, and in the imagination of the conservative Evangelical world in which he was formed. Smyth may have known full well that his actions were incompatible with the Christian faith but nevertheless used theology as a tool to groom his victims. Or he may have genuinely believed he was being a good spiritual father, disciplining young men and preparing them for a lifetime of being soldiers for Jesus in a war with the world. We will never know, but I am left intrigued by the question of how this spiritual and theological abuse could have been avoided. Graystone explains:

> Smyth's activities emerged in a context that was underpinned by theology and protected by culture that was entirely dependent on distorted notions of God, of spiritual ambition, and what it meant to be saved ... I have tried to understand how an organisation of individuals prepared to commit their entire lives unconditionally to Jesus could create a culture so toxic. The answers are a rich mix of power and human weakness, nurtured by a distinctive theology of shame and redemption ...[10]

Graystone speaks to how certain forms of theology lay the groundwork for the abuse Smyth sought to undertake in his home and in the camps he helped to run. The risks of spiritual abuse can be traced across theological and spiritual contexts, so this is not to suggest that conservative Evangelical theology is alone in having this issue. But it should be clear that theories of atonement, sacrifice and suffering are directly implicated in the abuse Smyth carried out on boys in his care. Though the results in this case have been extreme to many of us, we should be aware that more subtle forms of this kind of manipulation can be present in churches all over this country and the world. Where theologies valorize suffering and sacrifice and refuse to recognize human agency and dignity, the scene is set for abusers to take advantage. This abuse may not be comparable to the physical abuse seen in this case, but may manifest in financial abuse, demands for unpaid labour and excessive commitment to a leader or cause in ways that negatively impact health or wider relationships. Where one's faith has to be proven by what one is willing to endure for a 'good' or 'godly' cause, we can be sure that the risk of abuse is heightened.

What we also learn in the case of John Smyth is that systems and institutions that wield great power are no respecters of persons. We might have imagined, prior to this, that such an upper-middle-class institution is full to the brim of boys and men who only know privilege in many intersecting forms. But in this kind of context, designed by and for white male power, even those who might benefit might also fall victim. Graystone's analysis is not lost on me, that '[The victims] had been tightly bound through years of boarding school into a web of loyalty – to Smyth, to Iwerne [the network] to the reputation of their families and their school.'[11] While race, class and gender actively work against those of us who are women, from minoritized ethnic groups or working-class backgrounds, being white, male and upper-middle-class does not mean freedom from the risk of abuse. Power evolves and changes in different contexts and is dependent on the bodies in a room. In this case, the status of Smyth as an older, well-connected and trusted figure in the wider community enabled him to abuse those who, in his privileged world, were vulnerable.

At the same time, we cannot overlook the fact that at the point at which it was discovered he was a known abuser, he was allowed to leave the country for southern Africa. Clearly, he was able to abuse boys in the UK with impunity for too long, and was protected by those who failed to report him to the police. Why would a known abuser not simply be removed from post, reported and banned from 'ministering' anywhere? Why enable him to go to Africa to do further harm? Smyth himself asserts that it was God who called him to Zimbabwe,[12] but by all other accounts he was forced to leave by the Iwerne Trust. Smyth was sure to ruin their established reputation as a righteous and upstanding Christian organization fighting for biblical morality. He needed to be removed as far away as possible. But what of the communities and boys of Zimbabwe, who would receive this man, with no warning that he was an abuser, a wolf come to devour the sheep? While the evidence provided to the various reviewers suggests at least 30 boys in the UK suffered at his hands, this number was tripled during his years in Zimbabwe.[13]

It was in Zimbabwe that Smyth would be exposed more publicly although, in the end, he would avoid answering for his crimes. In Zimbabwe, Smyth abused boys younger than those at the Iwerne camps. One mother, on hearing her son's accounts, collated testimonies from other parents and boys and began legal action against Smyth. Her lawyer soon started to join the dots with Smyth's abuse in the UK. Local pastors organized together to compile evidence against Smyth, as they were hearing reports about the beatings.[14] When confronted, Smyth threatened to sue the local pastors, and convinced others there was a personal vendetta against him. Despite Smyth using his privileged position to obtain a permanent visa, lobby people within the government and hire lawyers to defend him, the pressure continued to build. The director of public prosecutions recommended he be charged with grievous bodily harm in relation to the boys who testified and manslaughter in relation to the death of Guide Nyachuru. Smyth was tried, but used his legal skills to derail the case. No evidence about Guide or the beatings was heard and the trial was inconclusive.[15]

Smyth, now deceased, was able to get away with years of abuse in the UK and Zimbabwe through manipulation of theology, his victims and the powerful people in his social circle. He clearly believed there to be one set of rules for the boys in his care, and one for him. He who sought to be the spiritual guide, responsible for forming endurance and faithful commitment in others, refused at every turn to be held accountable for his own actions. When faced with the harm he did, he blamed 'a mental breakdown' or changed the conversation to make himself out to be the victim. On the whole, he was a manipulator, an abuser who should never have been allowed near any pastoral setting with anyone, let alone children and young people.

Beyond suffering: A womanist response

The potential for atonement theories and theologies of suffering to contribute to Christian abuse has long been explored in Black, feminist and womanist theologies. Theodicy – theology of suffering – has particular importance in these traditions because they are born out of the existential crises faced by oppressed groups. The question 'Is God a white racist?', which titled William R. Jones's landmark 1998 book,[16] is asked because of the conundrum that emerges when Christian theologians' claims regarding a sovereign, loving and all-powerful God are brought into dialogue with the history of the enslavement of Africans and subsequent struggles for the fullness of life. This is even more of a poignant question since Christians – including ordained priests and preachers – were so deeply involved in the enslaving. They justified this violence as a divine order, and believed it to be necessary and good to exploit the bodies and labour of Africans. Why do we – as Black people – suffer seemingly incessantly, when God is supposed to love us and also love justice? This is the question Black theologians have sought to examine. For feminists of all ilks, the question of why women suffer in families, society or churches has prompted questions about whether a father God and his son care about – and can save – women at all. Latina, Asian and Black feminists/womanists have held gender and race together in their theological enquiries, asking why, even in the context of our own families, or churches that seek to serve communities of colour – at least in theory – women continue to suffer. Where do women of colour find refuge, when neither white-dominated societies and institutions nor our own offer us a place to lay our heads?

Evangelical theology has deep roots within Black communities around the world due to the history of Evangelical missionary work across the globe. Benefitting from the establishment of colonial ties, missionaries from Europe could easily travel around the world bringing their particular brand of Christian, Evangelical faith. The emphasis on personal encounters with God and individual conversion represented a significant shift for those whose cultures promoted a more communal understanding of spirituality and faith. This individualized faith included anxieties about individual purity and the salvation of the individual. With this came a particular theological emphasis on the Cross and suffering as core to Christian discipleship. Depending on the penal substitutionary atonement theory of the Reformers, the torture and death of Jesus are believed to have been a necessary sacrifice to pay the price for human sin. God shows us mercy by providing Jesus as our substitution after righteously judging us as guilty. Pioneering womanist theologian Delores Williams explains in *Sisters in the Wilderness* that to label Jesus as a 'substitution' is to see him as a surrogate figure, which sacralises the surrogacy roles Black women were forced into during slavery. Whether or not this is the intention, by talking about the goodness of Jesus' death 'in our place', Williams suggests an impetus was provided for those who spiritualized their abuse of Black women who were forced to be pregnant, to deliver and nurse babies, and labour in fields. This is, for Williams, a good enough reason to abandon this reading of the Cross altogether. Instead Williams asserts that:

to respond meaningfully to black women's historic experience of surrogacy oppression, the womanist theologian must show that redemption of humans can have nothing to do with any kind of surrogate or substitute role Jesus was reputed to have played in a bloody act that supposedly gained victory over sin/evil.[17]

Williams' argument highlights for us that all theories of atonement are formed by theologians who choose the biblical framework that resonates with them in light of their experiences. This is coupled with the appropriation of particular kinds of language and the cultural and social norms of their day. So too then womanist theologians must do the same in our context by thinking through the images, interpretations and emphases they must choose in light of Black women's collective experiences. Knowing, as Black women do, what it means to be forced to suffer in the place of another, makes it impossible, for Williams, to use this idea as salvific. God's love and plan to restore fullness of life to all creation cannot, in her view, come through the 'death of God's innocent child on a cross erected by cruel imperialistic, patriarchal power'[18] because Black women know this kind of power only ever kills. The Cross can never represent love; it signifies 'the evil of humankind trying to kill the ministerial vision of life in relation that Jesus brought to humanity' or 'historical evil trying to defeat good'.[19] Salvation is assured, for Williams, through 'Jesus' life of resistance' and his ability to enable people to see themselves not through the lens of 'inherited cultural meanings' but by embracing 'a new identity shaped by the gospel ethics and worldview'.[20]

What Delores Williams teaches us, in her re-reading of the Cross and critique of historical approaches to atonement theory, is that we must in our day and time commit to thinking and where necessary rethinking what we do with the Cross. As it becomes clear that existing articulations are enabling abuse – in her case of enslaved African women in America – we must ask in which ways we need to be clearer or more precise or change what we say altogether. We see in the case of John Smyth how abusers can continue to draw on ideas of violent suffering as good and necessary for the Christian life, even in contexts very distinct from the ones Black and womanist theologians have had in mind. With the long history of atonement theories we have already seen, this is not necessarily about creating something new, but speaking with greater nuance and discernment of the things of old. Williams reminds us that we are responsible for reflecting on the kind of behaviour and living that our theologies enable. Once we see the connections, we must act to mitigate the harm, if we care at all for the human family to which we belong, and the people in our care.

Sacred bloodshed

For womanist theologian and ethicist JoAnne Marie Terrell, who recognizes the harmful ways the Cross has been weaponized against Black women, men and children, the answer is not necessarily found in abandoning the Cross as a symbol of salvation. For Terrell, the Cross functions in various ways in the context of African American faith experience which is marked by forced sacrifice and the shedding of innocent blood. Terrell acknowledges that the Early Christians appropriated Jesus' crucifixion to theologize regarding their own experiences of persecution and martyrdom, which then developed into a 'hermeneutics of sacrifice'.[21] By this Terrell means that the idea that sacrifice is a necessary, inevitable or even positive aspect of the Christian life became a lens through which people interpreted what was taking place in the Bible and the world. In turn, this hermeneutic has been taken up to reflect on the situation of oppressed Christians in the centuries afterwards, including African Americans during slavery. African Americans have adopted this hermeneutic as a means of holding on to possibilities for survival and redemption even while enduring the unimaginable horrors of slavery.

There is therefore, for Terrell, a complex relationship with the Cross which offers hope for redemption on one hand and a tool for oppression on the other. This is in part due to the matter of who is the one doing the hermeneutical work – the work of interpretation. In her view, African Americans have appropriated the violence of the Cross for their use – namely spiritual survival – as they imagined what resurrection hope could exist at the other side of their cross, or what holy work might be done in the midst of their suffering. But in the hands of the slavers, those in whose interest it was to maintain power over them, the hermeneutic of sacrifice was imposed to further subjugate them. Terrell highlights for us an important question, which equips us as we consider how theologies of suffering and sacrifice might be used helpfully or violently: is the interpretation of a person or group's suffering being led by them, or by those in whose interest it is to control and dominate them? While we may share Williams' concerns about the ways Jesus as a 'substitute' serves to validate violence against Black women in particular, Black women have equally clung to this notion to interpret their suffering, as dignified members of Christ's body. Terrell is willing to retain the Cross along with its message of sacrifice despite Williams' critique, because it remains important to African American believers. Reflecting on the sacrificial love of her mother and other Black women, she believes that atonement theories which recognize Jesus as a sacrifice enable us to recognize Black women as related to Jesus, and their blood as sacred. Since for the Early Church the Cross 'signified both a divine rejection of sacred violence and a call to a life of service within the community of believers',[22] so today it confirms that there is no need for further sacrifices of living beings or bloodshed.

Terrell, no doubt, provides a helpful assist to those who hope to retain the hermeneutic of sacrifice and suffering as essential to their reading of the Cross. But the question for me is, would John Smyth agree? Or better still, does Terrell's reading do enough – as I would say Williams does – to mitigate against the way abusers might use it to legitimize the suffering and bloodshed they inflict on others? I would say Terrell's discussion of atonement theory raises the essential point about the agency we have – or that is taken away from us – in the act of interpreting our experiences or the Bible in relation to them. Now, I do want to be clear in saying that no interpretation of the Bible or life happens in a vacuum; our interpretation is also influenced by our culture, traditions, experiences and training if we have had any. Even if I sit alone with my Bible I am shaped by others, past and present, even subconsciously. If I attempt to process an experience, whether good or bad, my thoughts are impacted by those around me who have socialized me and taught me what to expect. If I grew up in a context where women were overworked and uncared for, I will carry that with me as I reflect on the Bible, on my life, and on any decisions I have to make. But this is not the same thing as having our agency ignored or overridden.

Our agency is ignored – and we are set up for abuse – not simply by others being a voice shaping how we might interpret or think about a particular experience (as I say, this is a normal and inevitable part of being social creatures). The danger appears when an individual or individuals position themselves (or we are manipulated to position them) as *the* voice of authority we must take seriously above all others, even our own. When we are exhausted, or in pain physically or emotionally, or depressed, we are forced to ignore or deny those real experiences, in effect to gaslight ourselves. We are made to affirm the interpretation of the one who has put themselves above us, and to pretend and even say that we are pleased, willing and content. Like the victims of Smyth who were forced to accept lashings despite the fear, pain and despair it created in them, we are made to put on a brave face and retain the illusion that the interpretation being foisted upon us is acceptable.

I am struck that in the story of how Smyth's abuse in England was exposed, Mark Stibbe describes the impact of his morning quiet time, where he was meditating on Psalm 23. The same

Bible, used to impose a hermeneutic of sacrifice on him, now was the source of his empowerment and liberation. On reading 'the Lord is my shepherd. I shall lack nothing' and seeking to make sense of 'thy rod and thy staff comfort me', 'suddenly he was gripped with a sense that Smyth's use of the cane was out of character with the Good Shepherd he was reading about.'[23] Empowered to interpret his own experience as painful and abusive in light of the same Bible Smyth used, the outcome was the opposite – not oppression but freedom. Mark Stibbe, as he took space to recognize his own truth regarding his experience, rather than the theological narrative being imposed upon him, found his own path to freedom.

Terrell's reading of the Cross in African American experience helps us to recognize the importance of our agency in interpreting our experience theologically. But in the end, the notion that shed blood is holy feeds too quickly into the kind of narrative Smyth would have loved. Repenting 'to the point of shedding blood' was often cited by him, and so sacralizing blood that its shedding became sacramental may well have added even more impetus to his abusive acts. While blood itself may be considered holy, its shedding should, in my mind, be viewed as sacrilegious, if we hope to break the tie between atonement theologies and abuses of power.

For me, Williams' critical reflection on the Cross and atonement does not cause me to ignore the Cross, but it invites me to consider the Cross as an *interruption* of the redemptive life-giving work of God. As the Cross interrupted Jesus' life – a life which continues of course – so too abuses of power interrupt the lives of individuals, families and communities. This interruption may of course be kept private over hours, days, months or years but retains an earth-shattering power, especially for victims. The life-giving work comes to us when the sin is exposed and the truth is revealed. Though this is often experienced as an unwelcome interruption of the community – at least in terms of our perceptions of it – it is the only way to move from death to life.

Conclusion

I do not aim to give the impression that particular atonement theories are entirely to blame for the abuse some people enact within the Church. Smyth, like others, made a conscious choice to harm these boys and used theology to justify his behaviour. John Smyth is not alive to give an account of why he did what he did to countless boys across two continents. But I have sought to encourage us not to let theology off the hook, as we seek to name what has gone wrong in contexts of abuse. Though it might seem less controversial to blame individual failing in cases like this, the more important work is to identify the factors that played into this scenario so we can collectively be on our guard, theologically.

This collective vigilance is in part about theological ethical education where we teach preachers and leaders to understand how theology shapes how we live, what we accept as good and what we resist. But it is also about ensuring that people are empowered to be the authority in naming their suffering and pain. It is about ensuring those who attend churches, youth groups, women's events or any other activity are reminded in words and actions that being disciples of Jesus does not require laying down one's dignity to an abuser. It must be made clear what sacrifice and suffering in the Christian life do and do not mean. And we must equip people to recognize that God's pleasure in us is not dependent on our willingness to submit ourselves to harm at the hands of one who seeks to dominate and oppress us, even when they claim to do it in the name of God. God does not delight in the shedding of our blood, any more than he did in the torture and murder of Jesus.

Notes

1 For a helpful introduction, have a look at Ben Pugh, *Atonement Theories: A Way through the Maze* (Eugene, OR: Cascade Books, 2014).
2 For a focused study of stripping, nakedness and abuse, see David Tombs, *The Crucifixion of Jesus: Torture, Sexual Abuse, and the Scandal of the Cross* (Oxford: Taylor & Francis Group, 2022), 8–26; Jayme R. Reaves, David Tombs and Rocío Figueroa, eds, *When Did We See You Naked? Jesus as a Victim of Sexual Abuse* (London: SCM Press, 2021).
3 Channel 4, 'Police Investigate Alleged "Brutal Lashings" by Christian Leader', *Channel 4*, 2 February 2017, https://www.channel4.com/news/police-investigate-alleged-brutal-lashings-by-christian-leader (accessed 4.06.2024); Channel 4, 'Archbishop Apologises for Historic "Abuse": The Full Story', *Channel 4*, 2 February 2017, https://www.channel4.com/news/archbishop-apologises-for-historic-abuse-the-full-story (accessed 4.06.2024).
4 Shingai Nyoka and Lucy Fleming, 'I Blame the Church for my Brother's Death, Says Zimbabwean Sister of UK Child Abuser's Victim', *BBC News*, 14 November 2024, https://www.bbc.co.uk/news/articles/c62lr331lkzo (accessed 21.02.2025); Andrew Graystone, *Bleeding for Jesus: John Smyth and the Cult of the Iwerne Camps* (London: Darton, Longman and Todd, 2021), pp. 106–7.
5 This is also evident in the report by the independent reviewer: Keith Makin, 'Independent Learning Lessons Review – John Smyth QC (October 2024)', pp. 45, 242, https://www.churchofengland.org/sites/default/files/2024-11/independent-learning-lessons-review-john-smyth-qc-november-2024.pdf (accessed 14.11.2024).
6 Graystone, *Bleeding for Jesus*, p. 34.
7 2 Samuel 7.14: 'I will be his father, and he will be my son. When he does wrong, I will punish him with a rod wielded by men, with floggings inflicted by human hands.' Hebrews 12.4–11: 'In your struggle against sin, you have not yet resisted to the point of shedding your blood. And have you completely forgotten this word of encouragement that addresses you as a father addresses his son? It says, "My son, do not make light of the Lord's discipline, and do not lose heart when he rebukes you, because the Lord disciplines the one he loves, and he chastens everyone he accepts as his son." Endure hardship as discipline; God is treating you as his children. For what children are not disciplined by their father? If you are not disciplined – and everyone undergoes discipline – then you are not legitimate, not true sons and daughters at all. Moreover, we have all had human fathers who

disciplined us and we respected them for it. How much more should we submit to the Father of spirits and live! They disciplined us for a little while as they thought best; but God disciplines us for our good, in order that we may share in his holiness. No discipline seems pleasant at the time, but painful. Later on, however, it produces a harvest of righteousness and peace for those who have been trained by it.' Proverbs 13.24: 'Whoever spares the rod hates their children, but the one who loves their children is careful to discipline them'; Graystone, *Bleeding for Jesus*, pp. 53, 59, 70.

  8 Graystone, *Bleeding for Jesus*, p. 59.

  9 Graystone, *Bleeding for Jesus*, p. 201.

  10 Graystone, *Bleeding for Jesus*, p. 8.

  11 Graystone, *Bleeding for Jesus*, p. 9.

  12 Channel 4, 'Christian Lawyer who "Beat Boys" was Charged over Zimbabwe Death', *Channel 4*, 3 February 2017, https://www.channel4.com/news/christian-lawyer-who-beat-boys-was-charged-over-zimbabwe-death (accessed 4.06.2024).

  13 Keith Makin, 'Independent Learning Lessons Review John Smyth QC', October 2024, https://www.churchofengland.org/sites/default/files/2024-11/independent-learning-lessons-review-john-smyth-qc-november-2024.pdf (accessed 14.11.2024).

  14 Graystone, *Bleeding for Jesus*, pp. 127–8.

  15 Graystone, *Bleeding for Jesus*, pp. 125–7.

  16 William R. Jones, *Is God a White Racist?: A Preamble to Black Theology* (Boston, MA: Beacon Press, 1998).

  17 Delores Williams, *Sisters in the Wilderness: The Challenge of Womanist God-Talk* (Maryknoll, NY: Orbis Books, 1993), p. 146.

  18 Williams, *Sisters in the Wilderness*, p. 146.

  19 Williams, *Sisters in the Wilderness*, p. 146.

  20 Williams, *Sisters in the Wilderness*, p. 145.

  21 JoAnne Marie Terrell, *Power in the Blood? The Cross in African American Experience* (Eugene, OR: Wipf & Stock, 1998), pp. 10–34.

  22 Terrell, *Power in the Blood?*, p. 33.

  23 Graystone, *Bleeding for Jesus*, p. 65.

6

The Problem of Vulnerability

Sometimes we are more afraid than we are actually vulnerable. (JoAnne Terrell)[1]

Defining vulnerability

Brené Brown has brought vulnerability back into the limelight in popular conversation, through her research on courage, shame, vulnerability and empathy. Her 2013 TED Talk 'The Power of Vulnerability' has 21 million views on YouTube, and she is a recognized voice on the intricacies of human emotion and relationships.[2] Brown is a trained social worker who seeks to make the complexities of human connection plain to us. She explains in her TED Talk that she collected thousands of pieces of data, and after writing on shame, then decided to focus on the participants she describes as having a 'strong sense of worthiness'. What they had in common was a sense of courage, compassion for themselves and others, and connection as a result of authenticity, and they fully embraced vulnerability. Vulnerability is lauded in Brown's work as an essential component of healthy relationships and good leadership. It is a way of connection, brought about by the honest bearing of our humanity, by allowing oneself to be willing to be 'seen fully'. Those 'wholehearted people', she explains, 'understood vulnerability as necessary, they were willing to say "I love you" first.' But while vulnerability may be necessary for connection, we are also deeply afraid of it. In her research, she discovered the many tactics we use to avoid it: we numb the feeling of being seen because of shame, and thus we numb so many other emotions including those we consider positive. In addition, we attempt to make certain those things which are uncertain – this includes, for Brown, rejecting open discussion in politics, or the unknown in our faith traditions – and we seek perfection in ourselves or others and we pretend that what we do doesn't have an impact on others.

Diane Langberg, an expert in abuse in religious contexts, follows a similar track by highlighting the vulnerability of being human. Vulnerability is, for Langberg, 'the capacity to be wounded', it 'leaves humans open to being blessed and hurt'.[3] In Langberg's view, vulnerability is not a choice we make, as Brown tends to focus on, but an inevitable aspect of our existence: 'Whether one sits on the throne of the Roman Empire or in the Papal seat, whether one leads a lucrative organisation or pastors a mega church, whether one is an undocumented migrant or a newborn babe, all are vulnerable all the time.'[4] This baseline understanding of vulnerability is important to enable us to develop empathy with those around us. There are common experiences we share in our relationships and in our lives in the world, and risk is one of them. We do not have control over all outcomes, we are at risk of harm, and we cannot move all things in line with our interests – we cannot even simply keep ourselves entirely safe.

But there are clearly dynamics at play which mean that while we might all share certain kinds of vulnerabilities in our humanity or interpersonal relationships, some have privileges that act as a buffer against additional issues. The leader of a 'lucrative organization' will experience fear about their child's future, like a parent in the inner city, but the nature and intensity of those fears will differ. We might all worry about whether we might find the right job, but some of us do not also have to worry about the racism, classism, misogyny, ableism or homophobia we might experience in the application process. The pastor of a megachurch may face some of the same vulnerabilities in terms of health as an undocumented migrant, but has the financial means to protect themselves against a huge number of risks. In a short and snappy definition which does not add more detail, we might be left to think that vulnerability impacts us all in the same ways, and thus we do not need to pay attention to the particular individuals or groups who face greater risks of harm. But this is also not free from complications. The definition of a 'vulnerable adult' is in statute and is crucial for safeguarding adults who are at particular risk of harm for a range of reasons. The need to pay particular attention to those recognized as being vulnerable should never be overlooked or sidestepped. However, in her work on the sexual abuse crisis in the Roman Catholic Church, Carolina Montero Orphanopoulos warns us that the term 'vulnerable adult' can be problematic: first, because it obscures human vulnerability as a 'universal anthropological trait', and second, because it situates the cause of abuse with the survivor.[5] In effect, if they were not vulnerable (it is implied), they would not have been abused. For Orphanopoulos, we should focus on the shared vulnerability we all have by virtue of being human, along with an awareness of the 'situational vulnerability' some may face due to the fact that 'every human being is not always equally vulnerable in different situations.'[6]

This matter of vulnerability differentials is front and centre in stories of abuse in the Church. But it is also the case that perceived vulnerability can mask the actual vulnerability we need to attend to. We can very easily misinterpret our own relation to power when we feel vulnerable. Our human frailty, the universal experience of vulnerability, can sometimes deceive us into underestimating the power we continue to hold – our situational power. This is exemplified very well when it comes to the question of gender, though it also plays out in other ways. Think about the 'Billy Graham rule'. For those who are not familiar, American Billy Graham is one of the most famous Evangelical preachers in the Church's history. In pursuit of what he called 'biblical integrity', Billy Graham set out a framework, which included a rule to not travel, meet or eat alone with any woman apart from his wife.[7] This has been praised and followed by many who view this as a sensible rule to avoid the risk of moral failure. It has also been heavily criticized for implying that women are the cause of men's sexual immorality and are constantly looking for opportunities to seduce 'godly' men. It has also enabled the old (and young) boys' club to continue by denying women access to mentorship, which, due to historic sexism in many churches, can only come from men. This kind of rule, I want to suggest, is born out of a failure to recognize our universal vulnerability – in which we all might be tempted to act out immorally – along with situational vulnerability. Graham and those who follow him focus on their own sense of vulnerability – maybe their own fear of succumbing to their sexual desires, or of being accused of having done so. But they fail to hold this together with awareness of the immense power they continue to hold in churches and Christian organizations. They overestimate their own vulnerability and underestimate the vulnerability of the women they encounter. By extension they focus entirely on self-protection and leave women exposed to further risk. If anyone needs rules to protect themselves in the Evangelical Christian world, where men have huge amounts of power, it is women. Even in cases where women have been sexually assaulted, it takes years for stories to emerge, if they ever do, due to systems that enable cover-ups, NDAs and individuals willing to do anything to protect the 'man of God'.[8] We have to learn to discern the difference between our sense of risk, our fear of certain potential outcomes, and the reality of the power we still have access to because of our name and reputation, or our gender, race, etc. This may mean that many will still give us the benefit of the doubt, even when we do not deserve it. In this case, we are not as vulnerable as we feel.

Second, displays of vulnerability can themselves be used in the power games some play, because they are aware of how vulnerability functions to build trust. Powerful figures can use emotion to consolidate power, using their tears or personal stories to encourage followers to let their guard down.⁹ Knowing how often we mirror the vulnerability others display, this can be a clever tactic to elicit personal information you would not usually share. When a person expects or demands your vulnerability in response to theirs, this is a clear red flag. A person who has huge power might hope to distract us from noticing it, by exaggerating their vulnerability. Leaders with huge influence can feign powerlessness and uncertainty, 'playing dumb' to avoid accountability. This can be used particularly by abusers who want to prevent themselves from being scrutinized or held accountable.¹⁰

Vulnerability is complicated. It is both inevitable and also constructed; defined by interpersonal and systemic factors; beautiful when it enables connection and tragic when abusers take advantage of it. We cannot simply laud it as positive or jettison it as problematic. And this complexity, revealed through those working within and beyond faith communities, is reflected in the theological framings we depend on to endorse it.

Why the 'servant leader' fails

We struggle to understand vulnerability and power in our interpersonal and social relationships, and this causes us one set of problems in our Christian contexts. But the problem of understanding vulnerability and power in the Church, especially as it relates to leaders, is exacerbated partly by the links we try to make between Christology, particularly the Incarnation, and Christian leadership ethics. In this central doctrine of the Christian faith, Christ who is God along with the Father and the Holy Spirit is born as a full human being. His mother Mary receives the Holy Spirit who 'overshadows her', enabling her to become pregnant with God in the flesh. Philippians 2 has become an important passage which forms a basis for understanding the Incarnation as an act of humility and vulnerability. It is here that we tend to root our ideas about humility and Christian leadership. The writer states in Philippians 2.5–8:

> In your relationships with one another, have the same mindset as Christ Jesus: Who, being in very nature God, did not consider equality with God something to be used to his own advantage; rather, he made himself nothing by taking the very nature of a servant, being made in human likeness. And being found in appearance as a man, he humbled himself by becoming obedient to death – even death on a cross!

The Greek phrase *ekénōsen heautón* is translated above as 'made himself nothing', but we often also find it written in English as 'emptied himself'. We can tend to skip over this, especially if we are familiar with the passage, but it is important to consider it because Philippians 2 is a central theological hook for discussions about Jesus' use of power. It is the only place we see this verb used and so much discussion has gone on about what it could possibly mean. This is even more of a challenge when there are not multiple uses to compare and contrast. Did Christ temporarily empty himself of some of his divinity when he was incarnated or did he pretend to, while keeping it all? Did he empty himself of the forms of 'worldly' power he could have used but which are contradictory to divine power? Or did he reveal, in his humility, that this is what God's power is like?[11]

Wherever we land on our understanding, I am concerned not so much with the various ways we might understand the idea of Christ 'emptying himself', but with the lessons we often draw from it. We have imagined, I think, that simply teaching people that Jesus emptied himself and was humble, and even *vulnerable*, would be sufficient to help leaders avoid abusive practices. Another commonly cited passage, equally powerful, is the story of Jesus washing the disciples' feet in John 13.1–17. Both of these passages at least in theory are supposed to adequately illustrate how Christians should and should not use power, and yet here we are. Some of those revealed to have abused power in horrendous ways will have read and preached these passages dozens of times. So what has gone wrong?

I do not think there is something particularly lacking in the relationship those who abuse their power have with the Bible. Each one of us falls short in varying degrees in terms of our capacity to be 'doers of the word' (James 1.22–25). But what concerns me is how by promoting 'servant leadership' as an ideal, we have simply created a narrative which in some cases acts as a cover for actions that are the very opposite. If I had a penny for every dominating male leader who claimed 'servant leadership' is what Christian leadership is about, I would be a wealthy woman. I want to suggest that this notion of servant leadership is not straightforward and is full of potential traps.

I am increasingly nervous about the 'what would Jesus do?' approach to the choices we have to make. I understand where it comes from. We encourage each other to follow Jesus' example in so many things, because he embodies goodness, righteousness and love. The writer to the Philippians instructs us to 'have the same mindset' as Jesus. Paul uses the metaphor of 'the body of Christ' to help us understand the spiritual connection we all have which is brought about through our faith in Christ and the work of the Spirit. We talk in common conversation about 'being the hands and feet of Jesus'. None of these ideas or statements are bad or unhelpful in themselves. But they can, when not accompanied by reality checks and honest reflection, trick us into thinking we are in some way replacing Jesus. Whether in our homes, churches and communities, we can start to think that in Jesus' physical absence, we must fill the gap.

To be clear, I believe fully in the Church as those whose lives are being formed as we follow in the way of Jesus. I believe that this formation, born out of true repentance, means we will live in ways that show signs of the way of Jesus, through the Spirit working within us. I believe that the Church is called to witness to the way of God, seen in Christ who made his home with the lonely and mistreated, and trusted in God's power even to the point of death. But I do not think Jesus needs to be replaced. I do not believe Jesus is dead, but that he is alive, continuing to lead us by the Spirit. We should not, in my view, be gathering people around ourselves as if we are Jesus, or taking pleasure in people seeking us out as a kind of celebrity. We are not the ultimate 'leader' if that is the language we want to use.[12] We are, if we have any power, simply holding a temporary position stewarding a power that does not belong to us.

Yet when we read Philippians 2 especially in relation to the task of leadership, leaders are often encouraged to see themselves as those who should mimic Jesus. The logic goes: if Jesus humbled himself and did not grasp on to power, then in your church or organization you, like Jesus, should be humble and not grasp. But if the leader is invited to identify as God in flesh, then it is too easy to end up seeing those they lead as just, well … flesh. The result is that the leader might practise humility, but from a position of imagining that, as in one reading of kenosis, they are almost playing pretend. A person may use the language of being 'empty' of power, adopt humble actions at least now and then, but still retain the sense of being something other than those they lead. They retain all the authority that comes with being the (or a) senior leader, and thus they can step in and out of humility and some forms of vulnerability, at any time. This problem of the servant leader paradox reflects a deeper problem of how we draw guidance for life from texts about an occurrence as unique as God becoming flesh. The challenge is inevitable when we attempt to create a human model out of a sacred mystery.

The danger of all of this is that we are trained to believe so much in the language and ideal of servant leadership that we fail to recognize and name the dynamics of power that are actually playing out. We hear a person use the key phrase, and as if hypnotized, we can slip into a kind of semi-consciousness. The language of 'servant leadership' can be a trap which encourages leaders to feign humility and vulnerability in order to conform to a Christian ideal, while retaining the power to dominate. They may find ways to switch between the two in a manner that makes it even more difficult to name the abuse. This may be because they are struggling to embody what is an oxymoronic notion. Or it may be because they want to keep hold of their power while using vulnerability to shield themselves from just critique.

But what difference would it make if instead of individualizing the notion of divine humility or 'emptying', we approached it as a community? The letter is written to the believers at Philippi, not to the 'leader(s)' after all. Similarly, Jesus, upon washing the feet of his disciples, tells them, 'Now that I, your Lord and Teacher, have washed your feet, you also should wash one another's feet' (John 13.14). This task is not given to one person to do over all the others; it is a communal responsibility to embody humility and vulnerability. The power of vulnerability may not be in the ways it enhances one individual's relationship to another. It may not be about how it helps us be the kind of leaders others can connect with. It may instead be in how we as a community, and as the body of Christ, become open to what we might gain when we refuse collectively to get one over on each other, even those beyond our group. The kind of vulnerability and non-grasping Jesus modelled, after all, involved being willing to look like he had lost, and that all was lost. It was a willingness not to fight for his own vision of what should happen, but to be obedient to the small foolishness of the kingdom that belongs to a child.

Jean Vanier and l'Arche

In light of the importance of looking at real-life cases, we will turn now to Jean Vanier and his sexual abuse of religious sisters (or nuns) over the course of his ministry. This is not a case from within the Charismatic or Evangelical worlds, but one that sent shockwaves through the wider Church where familiarity with Vanier and his work was extensive. I came across Jean Vanier and the l'Arche community as I began to become familiar with Roman Catholic social teaching and models of public ministry. Vanier was a well-known Swiss-born theologian and philosopher who founded l'Arche, a network of communities for those living with severe intellectual disabilities. The work started when in 1964 he invited two men with intellectual disabilities – Philippe and Raphael – to live with him in his home in a town north of Paris. There are now 149 communities in 39 countries on all five continents where people living with severe disabilities live with non-disabled assistants. Ten of these communities are in the UK. Vanier wrote many books on the theme of human vulnerability and disability, won significant grants and was regarded as a pioneering advocate for people with disabilities.

I met Vanier on a trip to the Taizé community in France. He came to speak to the hundreds of young adults who gathered and were hosted by the monastic community there, and I was sitting eagerly in the front row. As he walked in, the atmosphere changed and people fell quiet. He was unexpectedly tall, with a friendly face and warm countenance. At the time my French was good enough for me to understand him without the interpreter, and even to raise an eyebrow at a few interpretive choices I disagreed with. Sitting and listening to him was a beautiful spiritual experience. I felt God's presence in a way that was familiar to me and would be to many of us in the Charismatic world. I felt I had encountered a truly godly man, humble, kind and trustworthy. I was not prepared for what would emerge a few years later.

I remember when the story broke because the following week I was planning to teach a class using Vanier's commentary on the Gospel of John, his work on disability and the l'Arche community he founded. It came to light that he, along with his mentor Thomas Philippe, had sexually abused various lay women and religious sisters in the course of their 'ministry'. The initial summary report produced by l'Arche in February 2020 stated that allegations had emerged against Philippe in 2014 and were confirmed in 2015 after a canonical inquiry. Vanier claimed in 2015 and 2016 not to have known of Philippe's misdeeds, despite Philippe being sanctioned in 1956. In 2016 l'Arche received its first complaint against Vanier, which was investigated, but he claimed the relationship was 'reciprocal'. After a second allegation in 2019, l'Arche launched an independent inquiry. With both men dead by this point, investigations depended on the men's personal papers, and the testimonies of survivors, colleagues and witnesses.

The 2020 report explained that the inquiry team 'received six allegations from alleged victims and directly interviewed five of the women'. The investigation of allegations of sexual abuse revealed:

> The relationships involved various kinds of sexual behavior often combined with so called 'mystical and spiritual' justifications for this conduct. The relationships were alleged to have taken place under conditions the inquiry team label as 'psychological hold' and are described as emotionally abusive and characterised by significant imbalances of power, whereby the alleged victims felt deprived of their free will and so the sexual activity was coerced or took place under coercive conditions. This includes allegations that some of the sexual activity took place within the context of spiritual accompaniment whereby Jean Vanier, as a person of significant power and authority, would offer guidance to certain assistants he chose to accompany. Several of the women stated that they were vulnerable at the time and Jean Vanier was aware of this.[13]

The testimonies spanned 30 years and involved, as with all cases of spiritual abuse, the weaponizing of theology and misuse of Scripture. These women were single, married or vowed celibate and were coerced into sexual relationships by a trusted spiritual figure. Philippe was known to have developed an incestuous theology of the relationship between Mary and Jesus as this was used to justify his sexual abuse of women. He was ostracized by the Church because of his views and the reports of two women he abused in 1951. He put Vanier in charge of l'Eau Vive community which Philippe ran and used to cover his abuse, and Vanier allowed him to continue running it informally despite Philippe being banned from ministry by the Roman Catholic Church. The two men maintained a 'deep bond'. Vanier used the Song of Solomon to justify his abuse and place it on a pedestal in contrast to one woman's consensual sexual relationship with her partner.[14]

We would learn from the later Study Commission report published in 2023 that at least 25 women have come forward with testimonies of abuse by Philippe and Vanier.[15] In this interdisciplinary analysis of Jean Vanier, his mentor Philippe and the stories of survivors, we find a chapter on Vanier's spiritual writings and a theological analysis. Practical theologian Gwennola Rimbaut seeks to identify the writings that laid the groundwork for his abuse. She explains how, in his writing, Vanier referred to Scriptures less and less and promoted his own 'imaginative interpretation', sometimes adding details as if they were in the Bible when they were not. Despite having no training in biblical studies or theology, he felt comfortable making assertions without clarifying that they were simply his own musings. Vanier would often write of covenantal bonds and communion in ever-expansive ways. He valorized weakness or vulnerability and our embracing of them in others as a mark of true connection.[16] He focused considerably on marriage imagery and sexual intimacy as metaphors for spiritual union. He emphasized physicality and touching in writings, particularly in reflecting on caring for those with severe mental and intellectual disabilities. Rimbaut writes, 'This role of the body, beneficial at first, becomes the vector of all possible excesses if we do not use our discernment to qualify it. Yet, J. Vanier does no such thing when he talks about touching the bodies of people with disabilities.'

THE PROBLEM OF VULNERABILITY

Then she quotes him:

Mary held in her arms a little child who was her God. In this there is a mystery about the Body of Jesus, a mystery of touching which I understood a bit better by touching Eric's body, by washing him, holding him with respect and tenderness, because his body was the temple of God. I talked to him, but he was deaf and did not hear me, therefore my gestures were a way of communicating with him. At L'Arche, we are very sensitive to this mystery of the Body of Jesus, since many men and women of L'Arche do not understand speech.[17]

It is sickening to read these words, especially when we reflect on what we now know of his abusive practices. Both the 2020 and 2023 reports assert plainly that there have been no reports of Vanier abusing people with disabilities, and we all hope this reflects reality. But of course in a community where many individuals live with significant disabilities and where theological concepts involving communion, covenant and embodiment are central, it seems hard to be certain that potential instances of abuse would be disclosed or recognized.

Surviving Vanier

Reading Jean Vanier's commentary on John with fresh eyes, I am struck by the risks that now accompany perspectives I once thought only beautiful. And in addition are certain statements that hide some problematic views in plain sight. His emphasis on intimate touch, the valorizing of weakness and vulnerability alongside the focus on spiritual parenting is stark. Reflecting on Jesus healing the blind man, he writes:

Jesus, the compassionate one, touches the man. He heals not only through the word but through his touch ... Touch is the first and foremost of our five senses. It is the sense of love, for it implies presence, proximity and tenderness ... Tenderness never hurts or destroys the weak and the vulnerable, but reveals to them their value and beauty. It implies respect.[18]

He goes on to suppose that Jesus may have been involved in bathing Lazarus who he argues was disabled: 'The words of his sister, "the one you love is sick," seems to me significant. To me, these words imply "the one that you visit and bathe, the one you love with tenderness and affection, is in danger of death."'[19]

And finally, he holds up individual spiritual parenthood as the model for spiritual growth:

> Shepherding is about caring for those who are weak, lost and in need. It is about presence, love and support ... All of us who want to deepen spiritually and grow in a life of love and prayer need a spiritual father or mother who will help us on this road.[20]

We are faced with what to do with the writings or other resources of those who abuse their power in the Church. In the week the story broke, I opened up space for a rigorous debate about this with students where we could air feelings and critical perspectives on what to do with Vanier and others. Do we burn all his work, considering it corrupted beyond repair? Do we attempt to separate the author from the works to keep drawing what we can from them as if we never knew? We decided we would still read them, and dedicate time to thinking about how authorial intent, power and privilege shape the theology we and others produce. We asked ourselves whether in light of what may have been Vanier's intention, we can trust the idea that vulnerability, intimacy and communion are inherently good. And if not, what can keep us and others safe?

There are important theological lessons to be learnt here before we think finally about the practical question of boundaries. First is the notion of spiritual fatherhood that caused Vanier to cling to Thomas Philippe, a known abuser who was ostracized by the Church. Philippe was the most important theological and spiritual influence on Vanier, so much so that he compares their meeting to that of Jesus calling his disciples.[21] He goes on to say that this relationship was the reason why l'Arche began. We have seen in other examples, particularly John Smyth, how the notion of spiritual fatherhood is so easily weaponized to enable abuse. This can be the case for all of us, especially when we find ourselves in a particularly difficult time in our lives. But this is especially true for those of us who experience additional kinds of vulnerability due to our social dynamics around gender, age, etc. We might even consider Vanier, a younger, untrained layperson, as vulnerable to Philippe's particular model of spiritual guidance. Philippe was a spiritual director for Pauline Vanier, Jean's mother, and so there was also a close family connection. Vanier demonstrated a propensity for following in the footsteps of men he admired, as seen in his desire to follow his biological father into the military. He felt the sadness of being separated from his family while at boarding school and serving in the military. It is unsurprising that he would remain loyal to Philippe given this background. Nevertheless, even though he may have been groomed to be Philippe's spiritually abusive son, at a certain point he embraced what the Church had categorically condemned, and is fully responsible for the actions he took as a result.

The second issue we have here is the sacralizing of weakness and vulnerability, which portrays them as inherently virtuous states. Vanier's theologies of disability have been important for me, as for many others, for the way he seeks to recognize the dignity of those living with disabilities and value them as teachers, not simply as those needing care. This is essential for us all to grasp. But the problem, I think, is that in speaking of weakness and vulnerability as virtues, we fail to adequately assess the dangers and risks that accompany life as a severely disabled person. Vanier is interpreting the expressions of those he cares for – taking Eric as an example – but how does he know how Eric is experiencing being bathed by Vanier? We are not given access to Eric's own voice, nor can we get a sense of Eric's agency. Vanier may be gaining some spiritual revelation from bathing Eric – and claiming Jesus may have bathed Lazarus – but do Eric (or Lazarus) want to be bathed in this way? We are asked to take Vanier's word on the matter, with no possibility of a contradiction. By celebrating vulnerability, without paying adequate attention to the risks because of the dynamics of power at play, Vanier – whether intentionally or not – lays the groundwork for exploitation.

Finally, we have the problem of the body, yet again, but in a very different way to what we have seen so far. Vanier's case is different to many of the others we have seen which fall within the Protestant Evangelical and Pentecostal worlds. In those parts of the Church, the relationship between us and our bodies is fraught with suspicion and concerned primarily with discipline, control and even suppression. We saw how this played out with John Smyth and the Iwerne camps. In other parts of the Church, the relationship with the body is in my experience more nuanced. This is especially true when embodiment is embraced due to the centring of incarnational theologies. These enable us to celebrate our bodies and counteract the suspicion of the flesh. If the risks of bodily suppression are made clear in the case of Smyth, then Vanier exemplifies the dangers that lie at the other extreme. In his world, there is what we might consider an obsession with the body and touch as the primary sites of encounters between people, and between people and God. Because of this, boundaries which protect are not considered. And resistance to touch or bodily encounter can easily be framed as faithlessness. We can only imagine how sacralizing the body in this way would have enabled Vanier to manipulate the women he abused. Vanier, a charismatic figure (personality-wise), was considered a 'living saint' by many. But he also constructed – or simply utilized due to the influence of Thomas Philippe – a whole narrative as to why sexual abuse was theologically acceptable and spiritually necessary. The veneration of the body and touch, and the distortion of body theology, helped lay the groundwork for his abuse.

Boundaries are holy

Talk about vulnerability and weakness must be adequately nuanced if we are to avoid assisting those who seek to take advantage of others. We cannot outright ignore our inherent vulnerabilities as humans, but neither should we downplay the particular vulnerabilities and forms of power certain people have. This is especially true for those in positions of leadership who might minimize either their vulnerability or their power, whether deliberately or unintentionally through a lack of critical reflection.

What we need to take from Philippians 2, I think, is the importance of an honest appraisal of the powers and privileges we actually have, in any given context. The writer describes Christ first and foremost as 'being in very nature God'. There is a clear appraisal of who Jesus actually is despite the form he takes which could deceive us into thinking he is just a human servant or slave. Jesus is human, but he is God, and Philippians reminds us we should not forget that. Similarly, the story of Jesus washing the disciples' feet is preceded by 'Jesus knew that the Father had put all things under his power'. Jesus is clear about who he is, despite his human frame, his hunger, his need to sleep and physically rest. He is one who 'speaks with authority', he owns the power he has been given. He does not pretend he has no power when he is caught in a storm with his disciples and they panic. He does not act coy when the crowds come to him wanting to be healed. He knows the power he has, what he is supposed to use it for, and when he needs to give others space to play their role in meeting their own needs and those of others.

I am not encouraging us to put ourselves in Jesus' shoes here, but I am saying that we also need to be able to honestly assess the power we have. We do not want to fail to fulfil our duties, nor do we want to overstep. We do not want to bask in the privileges gained through 'race', gender, class, sexuality, etc., nor do we want to ignore them and pretend they don't exist. We must become power experts – being able to recognize and name our powers and privileges and how, even without us intending it, we might be engaged in dynamics of power which might easily become abusive. This enables us to set boundaries to keep others and ourselves safe from abuse.

One area in which significant thought has been given to the question of power and boundaries is in the area of counselling and pastoral care. In the context of a relationship between a pastor, a therapist or a counsellor, and the one seeking help, vulnerability and power are not straightforward. The care provider can feel deeply afraid of saying something wrong, causing a negative impact, or even facing legal action regarding an innocent mistake or misunderstanding. They may worry about being out of their depth when faced with a scenario they do not feel equipped to address.[22] The threat of professional or legal consequences is a genuine possibility and vulnerability. But the fear of a hypothetical scenario, the fear that you might make a mistake or not be as good a pastor as you think, is different from being in the position of having a crisis happening in real time that you are coming to someone to process or resolve. The difference between *hypothetical* and *actual* vulnerability needs to feature more in our analysis of vulnerability and power. You might be afraid of the possibility of coming across badly, but the person needing care has much bigger and more tangible issues at stake. Jan Berry, in her analysis of boundaries, power and vulnerability, explains it this way regarding training for ministers:

> I am concerned that often there is a focus on policies and procedures which bypasses the need for self-awareness and an understanding of the power dynamics implicit in the pastoral relationship. In practice, although I realize this is

THE PROBLEM OF VULNERABILITY

not the intention, this can result in an attitude of self-protection, in which the main concern of the recipient is to guard themselves against suspicion or false accusation. It can also have the result that there is an over-emphasis on rules and regulations, leading to a lack of empathy, or of flexibility and freedom within a relationship.[23]

The need for appropriate boundaries will be obvious to anyone with pastoral care experience. But this can primarily be focused on self-protection. As with all caring professions, there is a need to ensure the ones caring are not burnt out and exhausted. But beyond the practical questions of sustainability, it is important to remember again that even Jesus, God in flesh, took time to recognize his power, and also understood the importance of boundaries. I am intrigued by how respectful Jesus is of other people's right to consent, and to withhold consent.

Despite his divinity, good intentions and love, Jesus did not justify trespassing in relation to the boundaries of others, including those who were sick or living with a disability. He consistently asks those who are blind, 'What do you want?' And only offers healing when he is invited to bestow it. He even has to be convinced at times, demonstrating a strong commitment to honouring his own boundaries. This should be a stark warning to those of us who imagine that having good intentions rids us of responsibility for discerning the impact of our actions and behaviour. Care by consent – not a reluctant, but an enthusiastic, yes – is an important thread in the power–vulnerability conversation. We commit to gaining consent from the other person or people when we reflect and understand that we have power, and the potential to abuse it. This might be the power of being considered an 'expert' in your subject in a context where others would not see themselves as such. It might be the power of being white in contexts where white supremacy has historically taken hold. It might mean the power of being a man in contexts where masculinity is held up as the ideal form of humanity that must lead and instruct and define all others. It might be the power you gain from the accent, wealth, relationships or experiences you have due to your class background. There are many more. True consent is only given when there is no fear attached to declining and a deep sense that a yes will be good for you. Anything less is coercion, manipulation and an abuse of power.

But there is much we can learn from the people Jesus encounters – and this is important as we try to avoid thinking about ourselves as being replacements for Jesus. They do not simply give in to Jesus just because it's him. On several occasions, we find people setting their own boundaries around what they will or will not accept from him, and even pushing Jesus by asserting their own voice. We see this in the story of the Syrophoenician woman who does not let Jesus get away with not healing her daughter. She stands her ground and insists on what she needs, even in the face of Jesus' dismissive words (Mark 7.24–30). Similarly, people express clear expectations of him and negotiate boundaries. When Jesus asks whether he should go to the house of the Roman centurion to heal his servant, he refuses and instead replies, 'Just say the word, and my servant will be healed' (Matt. 8.8). This is, to me, the essence of Jesus' own vulnerability, that each time he asks, he may be denied. Jesus is not guaranteed welcome, embrace or acceptance, even among his own. And this humility, if anything, is what we might learn to understand and accept more gracefully through his example.

Notes

1 KoinoniaFCCBC, 'Final Lesson on Jesus and Power – Rev Dr JoAnne Marie Terrell 2-23-2014', *YouTube*, 25 February 2014, https://www.youtube.com/watch?v=gL_t1mooqgo (accessed 18.06.2024).

2 Brené Brown, 'The Power of Vulnerability', TED Talk, *YouTube*, 3 January 2011, https://www.youtube.com/watch?v=iCvmsMzlF70&t=217s (accessed 25.06.2024).

3 Diane Langberg, *Redeeming Power: Understanding Authority and Abuse in the Church* (Grand Rapids, MI: Brazos Press, 2020), p. 19.

4 Langberg, *Redeeming Power*, p. 19.

5 Carolina Montero Orphanopoulos, 'Vulnerability, Ecclesial Abuse, and "Vulnerable Adults"', in *Doing Theology and Theological Ethics in the Face of the Abuse Crisis* (Eugene, OR: Wipf & Stock, 2023), p. 28.

6 Orphanopoulos, 'Vulnerability, Ecclesial Abuse, and "Vulnerable Adults"', p. 30.

7 Billy Graham Evangelistic Association, 'What's the Billy Graham Rule?', *Billy Graham*, https://billygraham.org/story/the-modesto-manifesto-a-declaration-of-biblical-integrity/ (accessed 28.11.2024).

8 The cases of Ravi Zacharias and Bill Hybels are core examples of this. In both cases, they cited adhering to the Billy Graham Rule while also abusing women they encountered in the course of their ministry. Their respective organizations failed to deal with the allegations against them for years. See Rosie Dawson, '"Good and Godly Man" Ravi Zacharias Sexually Abused Women', *Religion Media Centre*, 15 February 2021, https://religionmediacentre.org.uk/news/good-and-godly-man-ravi-zacharias-sexually-abused-women/ (accessed 11.12.2024); Kelsey Hanson Woodruff, 'A Calculated Attack on Clergy Abuse: Challenging Patriarchal Power at Willow Creek Community Church,' *Theology & Sexuality*, 30:1 (2024), pp. 32–49, https://doi.org/10.1080/13558358.2023.2299187; Overthinking Christian Blog, 'Church Abuse, Non-Disclosure Agreements, and the Billy Graham Rule: An Interview with Laura Barringer', *Overthinking Christian*, https://overthinkingchristian.com/2021/05/26/church-abuse-non-disclosure-agreements-and-the-billy-graham-rule-an-interview-with-laura-barringer/ (accessed 11.12.2024).

9 I was struck by this when considering the comments made about Carl Lentz in the documentary *Hillsong*, where people who had suffered under a dominating and unjust church culture he presided over spoke about his frequent crying during sermons and displays of emotional vulnerability.

10 Some would consider the case of now ex-BBC broadcaster Huw Edwards to fall into this category. He has been charged with, and pled guilty to, making (i.e. accessing copies of) indecent images of children, and we now know his alleged crimes were not made public because his wife reported he was having mental health issues.

11 Here I have borrowed Sarah Coakley's summary of various readings of kenosis in Sarah Coakley, *Powers and Submissions: Spirituality, Philosophy and Gender* (Oxford: Blackwell Publishing, 2006), p. 11.

12 For a very compelling account of why we might abandon 'leadership' language as a heresy, and take up the biblical language of

discipleship once again, see Justin Lewis-Anthony, *You are the Messiah and I Should Know: Why Leadership is a Myth (and Probably a Heresy)* (London: Bloomsbury, 2013).

13 L'Arche International, 'Summary Report', 22 February 2020, p. 5, https://www.larche.org/wp-content/uploads/documents/10181/2539004/Inquiry-Summary_Report-Final-2020_02_22-EN.pdf (accessed 5.08.2024).

14 L'Arche International, 'Summary Report', p. 6.

15 L'Arche Study Commission, 'Control and Abuse Investigation on Thomas Philippe, Jean Vanier and L'Arche (1950–2019)', pp. 753-6, https://commissiondetude-jeanvanier.org/commissiondetudeindependante2023-empriseetabus/wp-content/uploads/2023/01/Report_Control-and-Abuse_EN.pdf (accessed 5.08.2024).

16 L'Arche Study Commission, 'Control and Abuse Investigation', pp. 753–6.

17 L'Arche Study Commission, 'Control and Abuse Investigation', p. 762.

18 Jean Vanier, *Drawn into the Mystery of Jesus through the Gospel of John* (London: Darton, Longman and Todd, 2004), p. 174.

19 Vanier, *Drawn into the Mystery of Jesus*, p. 196.

20 Vanier, *Drawn into the Mystery of Jesus*, p. 174.

21 Vanier, *Drawn into the Mystery of Jesus*, pp. 41–2.

22 Jan Berry, 'A Safe Space for Healing: Boundaries, Power and Vulnerability in Pastoral Care', *Theology and Sexuality Journal*, 20:3 (2015), p. 209.

23 Berry, 'A Safe Space for Healing', p. 204.

7

The Power of Discernment

> May we all learn how to discern when power is being used wrongly and call it by its right name. (Diane Langberg)[1]

In the conclusion of her analysis of abuses of power in the Church, and how to prevent them, Diane Langberg calls us to learn to discern. This should not be read as a trivializing or clichéd response. Langberg names so many of the power issues we have seen throughout this book. She is unflinching in her naming of toxic theologies and the issues they cause. She boldly calls out narcissism and patterns of control and mistreatment. She does so not as a philosopher or even a theologian, but as someone who has committed her life to healing work with survivors of abuse. And when it all comes down to it, discernment, she says, is what we need.

In talking about discernment in this final chapter, we are of course talking about a spiritual practice, not just a theology. There are of course theologies of discernment – ideas about what discernment is in relation to God – but this is not the focus of this chapter. I do not think that simply addressing what I consider to be theological imbalances or errors is enough to deal with the abuses of theology, power and people that I have explored throughout this book. That is because these abuses, both for perpetrators and survivors, go beyond the intellectual. These disordered ways of thinking make their way into daily practices and habits that are spiritual, physical or embodied, theological, emotional, psychological, etc. But some of the root causes of abusive behaviour are not purely or even primarily theological. By this I do not mean to say they cannot be read theologically or that they are not undergirded by theology. I mean to say that the problems of power abuse involve other factors. Personal issues, habits of exploitation, misogynist or racist attitudes, narcissistic personality types, all have a major role to play in abuse. In other words, there is a particular kind of distorted formation that occurs as people twist theology for abusive means, or inhabit spaces where spiritual abuse is normalized. There must therefore be a counter-formation in the work of addressing spiritual abuse that goes beyond a purely rational, theological argument.

In contrast to what we might imagine when we hear the word 'discernment', this is not something reserved for a chosen few. The 'discernment process' is something I have come to be familiar with through my work in theological education with the Church of England. This process is focused on figuring out if God is calling a person to ordained ministry or a different vocation. The individual has a sense of call, but the wider community is also central to this. There are those who put the person forward, and those who encourage them to continue (or discourage them from doing so). And then those who begin to train the person to fulfil the calling they and others believe they have. Even at this point, discernment continues, and the person or those around them may come to the conclusion that this may not in fact be what they are called to. All churches and traditions have their own equivalent processes, whether formal or informal. They are designed to help churches and individuals judge which gifts have been given for ministry in a particular place.

Discernment can be focused on those exploring a calling to some particular ministry. But it is much broader than this. Discernment in the Bible and Christian tradition is a spiritual gift needed by all of us. There is of course a particular emphasis on those who have important responsibilities in the community or nation. This is understandable – we all need discernment as we lead our own lives, and those responsible for supporting others will inevitably need to exercise this even more. This includes those of us who are teachers, preachers, ministers, podcasters and writers, who shape the thoughts of others in more obvious ways. But it is also about parenting and being a good friend, it is about discerning what we put online, if or when we speak in a meeting, when we pull back or lean into a situation at work. As members of communities we need discernment in order to do our part in loving God, our neighbours and ourselves well, in the midst of complex and imperfect circumstances.

But speaking about discernment, especially in relation to navigating churches and contexts where abuses of power may occur, is not straightforward. This is because defining discernment is not simple. As we will see in the next section, a perusal of the Bible will reveal there is no one way of thinking of it. There are elements that can be taught and others that, seemingly, cannot be. It is given by God, but also something we have to cultivate, strive for and practise. It helps us know how to think (and not think) and also what to do (and not do) and to see ahead to the consequences. But it also involves spiritual dynamics – it enables us to identify spiritual presences and influences that exist behind human action.

In this final chapter, I will explore and hopefully unpick some of these tensions in order to tease out what it might mean for us to learn to discern. But I want to say first of all that this is not in any way meant to suggest that those of us who have survived abusive contexts are to blame for what we have experienced. The point of this chapter is not to evoke shame by suggesting that if only we had discerned better, everything would have been fine. We are not responsible for the abusive actions of others – they are. But I do think – and this may be cynical of me – that we will never arrive at a place when we can spot every abuser, or hold them to account. Many are very clever at disguising their behaviour, grooming communities to protect them even when accusations emerge. Many of us do not recognize our own tendencies to abuse power, or our closeness to doing so. We do not know what is in our own hearts often, and what may lurk within us, yet undiscovered. Since temptations abound for others and ourselves, and enemies continue to prowl back and forth looking to devour, we must equip ourselves, and those we care for and support in whatever capacity, to guard ourselves and others as much as possible.

Lack of discernment: A spiritual crisis

I do not imagine that many of us have been taught to discern. We have been encouraged to join rotas, to talk to God, to sing to God, and given a set of rules or expectations to live by in relation to our personal lives. We might have been taught to pray and intercede, to prophesy in a Charismatic setting, to preach or prepare a great sermon with engaging illustrations. But rarely have we been taught to discern. Instead, I suspect, many of us have been encouraged to depend on the discernment of others. We have been encouraged to trust others to discern for us – a pastor, a preacher, a theologian, a youth leader or a spiritual guide. Or we have been encouraged to see these people as discerning – whether they are or not – and thus to give them undue power to influence our lives. It is possible that we have, at least on some level, given over the responsibility of discernment, since learning to discern is not easy work. It is somewhat easier to let someone else do it, even if it is more risky. Either way, we have not been able to tune in to our own wisdom gifted to us by the Holy Spirit. This wisdom is formed in us as we reflect prayerfully alone or with others, with the help of the Scriptures, the faith-filled words of those who have gone before us, and our own experienced wisdom. We have been encouraged in some contexts to neglect our own spiritual gifts, and instead depend on others to guide us. This dependency we have been told, directly and indirectly, makes us good Christians, especially when we are women, young people, new believers or those deemed 'uneducated'.

There is of course an essential place for relationship in learning to discern, as we will see. From the start, we need others to encourage us and help us learn what discernment is. We are dependent on biblical writers, spiritual guides and teachers of the faith both living and now passed on. Discernment is inevitably communal. My earliest memories of thinking about discernment involve conversations with my mum and dad, as I listened to them process big decisions. In my church, we were regularly taught to 'test the spirits', which meant to discern whether an expression of spirituality was really from God or not. While community is important, sometimes when we find ourselves at a fork in the road in our own lives, or facing a painful situation we are trying to understand, we can overlook the wisdom that is within us. In rushing to hear what others might say, we forget that we are the experts in our own situation and experiences. We downplay the presence of the Spirit in our lives, who is in communion with our spirits, speaking, leading and guiding us even in ways that can seem undetectable. When we feel something might be 'off' with a person or situation, we can distrust our own intuitive wisdom, and allow others to convince us it isn't serious or doesn't need addressing. I have had too many experiences of being bombarded with the opinions of others, only to sit in meditative quietness, and feel those burdens fall away as my own voice and the quiet whisper of God become clear. I therefore hold it to be true that cultivating discernment depends on the support of the wider community, but we must also be discerning about the communities who shape us in this area. We also need to learn when to silence other voices and tune in to the voice of the Spirit guiding us. External voices can be useful to help inform our perspective and opinion. However, whatever we decide must also reveal itself to remain true, even as we sit alone away from the glare of others. We should not trust just anyone with the sacred task of helping us to discern and make decisions in our lives.

The lack of teaching in this area can lead to kinds of infantilization in our spiritual formation, which can be deliberate but in other cases it might not be. This dynamic of dependency on others and personal disempowerment has deeply formed the contexts in which many of our leaders have also been trained and developed. Some have not been equipped to think critically for themselves about their experiences, the Bible, or the culture of their faith community. Many of them were handed a list of doctrines and ethical demands and told this is what they should believe, at least to be part of a particular denomination or tradition. They were not encouraged to think critically and discern what might be true in their context and for their ministry, and so they can't teach us. They themselves may be suffering through their own lack of discernment. They are not equipped or allowed to discern for themselves the path they must take, and do not even know what it would mean to encourage that in others. Of course there are those who deliberately stifle the capacity of others to discern for themselves, through actively encouraging unhealthy models of dependency. This is a mechanism to enable abuse and exploitation, as we have seen in some of the cases throughout this book. But I do not think it is always as deliberate as we might think. So how might all of us be enabled to discern better?

Discernment in the Bible

As I have said, a precise definition of discernment is tricky, but we can get close to a sense of what it can mean in certain biblical texts. Discernment is often paired with wisdom. In the New Revised Standard Version, it occurs first when Joseph interprets Pharaoh's dream and advises him to select a 'discerning and wise' man to manage the national plan for the famine (Gen. 41.3). Discernment in this case is associated with knowing what to do when there are different options, and how to go about it. We then find references to discernment in relation to perceiving the result of a particular path (Deut. 32.29); telling the difference between 'good and evil' or 'pleasant and not' (2 Sam. 14.17, 19.17). Discernment is often attributed to

Solomon, known to be gifted with divine wisdom (1 Kings 3.9–12, 4.29). In these examples discernment is about foresight, and being able to distinguish between different kinds of things. We also see that a lack of discernment prevents a person from seeing clearly (Job 4.16); but having it enables you to learn important lessons (Prov. 17.10). It can be gained, given, lost or even taken away by God according to some biblical writers (1 Kings, 3.12; Prov. 1.5; Job 12.20). There are elements of discernment that are spiritually imparted, but it can also be sought out through focus and determination. But discernment is not just for people. God is described by the psalmist as being able to 'discern my thoughts from far away' (Ps. 139.2).

In the New Testament, Paul speaks of discernment in several of his letters. He encourages the church in Rome to 'discern what is the will of God'. For Paul, this depends on not being 'conformed to this age', but 'transformed by the renewing of the mind' (Rom. 12.2). Discernment is sharpened, then, when we resist ways of thinking and being that stand in opposition to the ways of Christ. We cannot discern well if our values and loves are not in order. Paul recognizes spiritual discernment as crucial to receiving and understanding spiritual gifts (1 Cor. 2.14). In other words, we need to be able to judge or determine which are genuine expressions of the Spirit's presence and which are not. We cannot assume that just because some spiritual expression *appears* to be of the Holy Spirit, that it is. Paul gives us the example of the need to determine who is 'speaking by the spirit of God' (1 Cor. 12.3) and who is not. We cannot simply switch off our discernment because we are among the community of believers – we must remain alert; not everything is as it seems. He also instructs the early believers to 'discern the body of Christ' when gathering to share in his supper (1 Cor. 11.29). Paul uses the 'body of Christ' as a metaphor for the Church. But since he is keen to emphasize that there is only one body – which is core to his point – we know he is not suggesting in 1 Corinthians 11 that there are two bodies of Christ (churches) to discern between. Although he also himself discerns between faithful believers and those who are not, here it would seem that 'discerning the body' is less about distinguishing and judging the church(es) and more about careful consideration of the actual body of Jesus, that was hung on a cross and is now resurrected. Of course biblical scholars and theologians continue to debate this and still do not agree. In 1 Corinthians 12.10, 'discernment of spirits' is named among the variety of gifts given by the Holy Spirit to believers. Paul expects discernment to go beyond the material realities of people, behaviours and attitudes, to the spiritual, invisible powers that might influence and shape what we can actually see. Discernment allows us to access knowledge that does not come to us through purely rational means.

Discernment and Christian tradition

I am a born and raised Pentecostal so will always look to this tradition as I ponder anything relating to spiritual gifts and formation. To speak about discernment as a gift of the Holy Spirit, available to each person, is important for all of us. Wherever we find ourselves on the spectrum of Christian tradition, we need this spiritual ability to judge between what is good and not, what is right and not, what is aligned with God's being and God's ways and what is not. But as we have seen, there are specific risks of power abuse in Charismatic and Pentecostal spaces due to the openness to spiritual expressions that can be easily manipulated. This does not necessarily mean we are *more* at risk in such contexts – individuals who spiritually abuse others will use whatever is at their disposal. But it does mean there are particular kinds of temptations we must be mindful of.

Nevertheless I am convinced that these traditions hold the cure, as well as contributing to the causes, regarding some of the theological and power abuse issues we have seen in these areas of the Church. While this democratizing of spiritual gifts means people with charismatic personalities can whip up a frenzy of popularity around themselves, it also means that everyone else, technically at least, has access to the same resources to resist such a trend. As I said previously, it was not uncommon for pastors in my home church growing up to remind us of the need to 'test the spirits'. This was a call to discernment. It was a reminder that we cannot simply take spiritual expressions at face value and presume they are from God. There are many spirits, some of which are opposed to God and yet function in the gathering of the saints. While Charismatic traditions awaken us to the Spirit's empowerment to speak prophetically, they also alert us to the Spirit giving us power to listen. Listening should, I think, be recognized as a spiritual gift even more so than speaking. It may well be implied through the focus on discernment – since it requires listening to God, ourselves and others as we seek to make right judgements. It is only through listening deeply enough and critically enough that we can judge what might really be considered a divine word or not.

Contrary to some of the more reductionist – and sometimes classist or racist – critiques of Pentecostalism, discernment has always been core to classical Pentecostal spirituality. For the churches born at or through the Azusa Street Revival from 1906, there was a clear understanding that discernment was essential to the lives of believers. The early records of the *Apostolic Faith* newspaper, written by the early leaders of the movement, demonstrate that these working-class, predominantly Black believers reasoned regarding theological dilemmas and were unafraid to speak decidedly about what they understood to be right and wrong regarding Christian beliefs and their practice. This included being able to name the racialized power games being played by those who wanted to undermine this multiracial congregation. From the outset Pentecostals in this particular context understood that spiritual gifts came with responsibilities. They recognized that conversation and dialogue was continually needed as people sought to live with the expectation of spiritual gifts while acknowledging the risks that could be involved. Discernment is a major part of what it means to embrace Charismatic traditions. It is not a box to be ticked once, but an ongoing spiritual practice that helps to safeguard the community as a whole and particular groups or individuals who are especially vulnerable.

My understanding of discernment is also informed by my subsequent experience of contemplative Christian spiritual practices. On a retreat run by a group of Roman Catholic sisters in London, I was first taught about attending to the rhythms of 'consolation' and 'desolation' that shape our lives. Drawing on the ancient spiritual wisdom of St Ignatius of Loyola, they highlighted ways we might figure out what to do, if anything, when faced with challenging situations. Ignatius includes a whole section on 'rules for the discernment of spirits' in his *Spiritual Exercises*, published in 1548. In it he helps believers recognize the presence of spiritual powers in and on their lives, through whether they find themselves in a place of consolation or desolation. Throughout his writing he speaks of 'consolation' as 'some interior movement in the soul' whereby a person is overcome with love for God and sees everything through the lens of this love. It is the experience of being full of gratitude, hope, joy, faith, peace, capacity for gentleness, patience and all the traits of a life full of the Spirit. It also includes tears of 'sorrow for one's sins' or tears that reflect 'the Passion of Christ our Lord'. This is what we hope to move towards. Desolation is what he uses to describe the opposite, the times when our inner lives are agitated or disturbed, when we experience 'movement to things low and earthly, the unquiet of different agitations and temptations, moving to want of confidence, without hope, without love, when one finds oneself all lazy, tepid, sad, and as if separated from his Creator and Lord.'[2] Here Ignatius invites us to discern through our bodies, our emotions, what we feel and what they might tell us about what is happening to us spiritually. We are taught sometimes to distrust our emotions, but they often play an important role in flagging something that needs attention. This can be true in terms of our spiritual lives, as Ignatius wants us to reflect on, as well as in our relationships, our working lives or other aspects of our lived experience. He warns us about making decisions when in a period of desolation, since we are more likely to be guided by bad spirits. Instead, we should hold fast to those things we knew to be true when we felt close to God and deeply connected to divine love.

Discerning today

Discernment in the Bible and in Christian tradition, if we attempt to sum it up, is about tuning in to divine guidance so that we might see a situation or reality clearly – as it is, not how we want it to be – and determine how to respond inwardly and outwardly. It can be summed up in the question 'What does God desire here?'[3] It is a manner of holding ourselves and others accountable to the greatest commandment, which is the sum of all others: to love God completely, and our neighbour as ourselves. The method of discernment is also born out of this same foundational Christian ethic. We cannot discern only as individuals attempting to gain divine wisdom with no communal dialogue and input. Discernment requires that we explore certain questions openly, with God and in conversation with others we can trust. It is an opportunity to weigh what we are sensing within ourselves and what others testify to from their own experiences and reflections.

This book has partly been an exercise in theological discernment. It has focused on exploring what is as it should be, and what is not, in our theologies and their consequences. It is an attempt to teach what can be passed on rationally, through reflection and critical analysis. We can learn some elements of discernment as we listen to those who have taken time to think deeply about these questions and who are motivated by love for all people. We learn discernment as we benefit from those who have deep knowledge – whether by lived experience or professional training – and can help us spot abusive behaviour in our midst.

But discernment is not purely rational or intellectual. It is a gift that is part of us, bodily, not just mentally, and we have to learn to tune in. We have talked about this as a spiritual gift, but that is not supposed to give the impression that it is something we can do by attempting to ignore the body and its wisdom.[4] In fact, sometimes our spirits and our bodies know something is wrong before our minds have a chance to catch up. For some, this might simply feel like an intuitive knowing or a gut feeling. We can discern as we pay attention to how a person or place makes us react. This is not enough in itself because our instinctive reactions to people are often shaped by prejudices. Discernment can of course fall into the trap of our biases and we must be on guard against this. It would be too easy for a man to always 'discern' that a woman was the issue, or for a white person to 'discern' that the Black man is up to no good, despite there being no real issues with their behaviour. This is partly why a trusted community, where we can be invited to reconsider our assumptions, is essential. But in a context where we too often do not believe a person or even give a fair hearing if there is not enough evidence, we do need to be reminded of the kinds of knowledge and insight we need and do not always value.

We should not simply follow these feelings, but if attended to properly, our embodied reactions can enable us to identify that something is not as it should be, in ourselves, or in the dynamic we are experiencing. As we start to sharpen this way of knowing, we can come to understand when we are really tapping into discernment or when we are simply projecting assumptions. We should be provoked by these reactions, to tune in and ask what our bodies are telling us. Do you tense up in the company of a particular person or feel nervous and afraid when they walk into a room? Or alternatively, is your nervous system calm and at ease when in a particular space?

And in addition, how do others react to that person or place? We might feel calm around someone, maybe because we share some identifying feature with them – but how do others react? Do all the men seem to get along with him well, but the women look uncomfortable – are they being silenced somehow? We can, I think, learn discernment as we experience what it feels like, in our own bodies, to be in particular situations. But we can learn a whole lot more by paying attention to what is felt by those who are not like us.

At times we can imagine – especially those of us who believe in spiritual gifts – that there is a fast track to learning to discern, but there is not. We have seen that discernment can be understood as given to us by God, but also that it is something we must nurture and practise. There are two important implications of recognizing discernment as both a divine gift and a spiritual skillset. First, we acknowledge that we cannot discern well without divine assistance. Second, we are reminded not to underestimate our need to intentionally practise this habit. Discernment is like a seed sown in us, that we must water, ensure it gets enough sunshine, and is protected from the frost. Recognizing we need to discern is therefore the first step in a journey of spiritual formation. The journey involves the cultivation of this gift through our practice.

Discernment and individuals

The practice of discernment is a habit of spiritual reflection whereby we bring spiritual wisdom to bear on the situations, responses and feelings that arise for us as we find ourselves in particular places. It is focused on the pursuit of truth, summed up in the questions 'What is going on?'; 'What is happening in this situation?'; 'What is at the root of what I can see here?'; 'Who is involved, and who if anyone is responsible?' This may not result in one overall truth, but sometimes in multiple truths.

Discernment is needed on several levels when it comes to cases of abusive behaviour by individuals, and the use of theology and spiritual language in that abuse. All of us must be discerning about the people we hold up as examples, whom we praise and endorse. This is a point of individual as well as communal reflection. We do not know people as well as we imagine, and we must accept this in order to recognize the need for discernment in the first place. Discernment is about right judgement – but if you think you already know a person or situation, why would you think you need to learn to judge better? This is often where the issues begin, with us being more certain than we should be about the people, places and patterns that play out in some of our Christian contexts. When the story emerges that a person has abused someone or a group over a period of time, we think back to our own experiences to corroborate the story. However, in reality, how we have experienced a person can have very little, and sometimes nothing at all, to do with what other people have encountered. This is especially the case when the 'others' are those with less privilege than us. When we hear that someone has had some level of theological or ministry training, we may begin to assume that they should be trusted. But having knowledge and deserving trust are two very different things. I can trust the facts you may have picked up through your education, but to trust you and what you do with that knowledge, I must know something more about your character. I must have a sense that you know your place and are not attempting to coerce or dominate me. I must know, through what I experience over time, that you are not seeking to take the place of God in my life or anywhere else.

But discernment is enabled in us not only through paying attention to those spaces that are harmful, but also through being in loving, healthy and safe environments. One of the reasons why I feel so strongly about toxic theologies, and the violent spaces they create, is because I know it doesn't have to be this way. I have worked in various Christian contexts and come away with glimpses of the good that is possible, as well as stories of what should never happen. Our hope is to reinforce and expand these signs of goodness. A priest, who treated me as a person called by God for a particular vocation that was yet to be understood, taught me to discern the difference between a trustworthy shepherd and an exploitative leader. A Roman Catholic nun who acted as my spiritual director expanded my understanding of God away from a demanding father who wanted me to produce for and please him, to that of a mother gazing kindly at me as I rested. She enabled me to discern the difference between a healthy spiritual environment and one that would eventually burn me out and leave me empty. My prayer is that each of us who has experienced spiritual trauma will be healed through the loving kindness of those who embody the pastoral care or simply the friendship we always hoped we would find in others. While harm can be done in our relationships as we journey in faith, so too can healing. This does not mean we will not carry scars, but simply that the wound, over time, may close up and be soothed.

As well as being discerning about who we trust and elevate, discernment is about distinguishing between what is worthy of praise in ourselves and others, and what is not. This requires us to see ourselves as we ought and not more highly (Rom. 12.3). It is the essence of humility. Some of us are inclined to let ourselves and others off the hook when we or they should be held accountable for wrongdoing. Others of us specialize in enacting harsh judgement on ourselves and others for simply being human. There is definitely a need to be gracious when we are dealing with nothing more than a human tendency to slip up and make an error. But this is not the same as someone who practises a habit of manipulation, mistreatment and bullying that spiritual abuse cases highlight. Discernment demands that we distinguish what can be tolerated without violating our responsibility to actively care for our neighbours and even our enemies, from what is unacceptable considering that responsibility. It requires us to act in solidarity with those feeling the force of this behaviour, and those who may not even be able to name it, but are being negatively affected. Discerning this involves asking about the impact this person, action or behaviour is having on others. And asking important questions about the use of coercion through fear and shame and the capacity to consent or withhold consent.

Discerning the powers

But good discernment goes beyond individual interpersonal issues and personal stories. This is why it is the case that simply teaching individuals to discern better will not solve abuses of power. We can try our best with Ignatian exercises, but will they enable us to identify, leave or change (where possible) abusive dynamics? We must also learn to recognize the sinfulness of the powers, systems and structures we accept, and sometimes sustain, if not actively then passively through our inaction. Surely these institutions and systems exist because of individuals, but so often they take on a life of their own. We might be actively working against patterns of sin, and yet they persist. They can be the outworking of our collective imagination which tells us either that this is how it should be, or that it can never change. Discernment is about recognizing when the powers are given over to evil, rather than mistaking them for good and godly authority. It means noticing when our motivations are disordered and we become complicit in what we should resist on a structural level for our sake and for the sake of those we are seeking to serve.

In his book *Engaging the Powers: Discernment and Resistance in a World of Domination*, Christian theologian and ethicist Walter Wink helps us to think about discernment beyond the interpersonal. In his series on 'the powers', he writes several books that take biblical, theological and ethical approaches to discussing power, oppression and injustice in the world. 'Spiritual discernment', he says, is crucial for the transformation of the powers – those forces described in the New Testament in many different ways. They tend to be visible, but can also be invisible, and in the case of visible institutions, structures, etc., they always have an inner spirituality. In some places they are described as divinely created, but in others as sinful, even demonic. For Wink, transformation is impossible if we do not pay attention to the spiritual inner dynamic, which must be spiritually discerned. He writes:

> There are no prepackaged answers that tell us how Christians should engage the powers. One person may be called to try to re-organise the office where she works in a more humane fashion; another may have to walk out to protest sexual harassment. One may run for political office; another may despair of the electoral system and work to overthrow it ... spiritual discernment takes the place of fixed rules.[5]

Here Wink reminds us that spiritual discernment always has good or right action as the objective. It is not simply accumulating wisdom for its own sake, but to enable faithful embodiment of the faith that is professed. Discernment is supposed to lead to seeing what is disruptive, difficult or awkward, for once we have a clearer sense of the truth, lies and deception are exposed. Discernment disturbs the powers, whether institutions, families or church groups, because it refuses to play along with the lie. This can be difficult to get our heads around since, as we saw in Chapter 4, so many of us are schooled to be discerning about those beyond the walls of the church but not those within it. But it is crucial that we reject the binary that prevents us utilizing spiritual gifts of discernment in the presumed sacred space.

Discerning spirits

No one really knows what to do with demons. They are an awkward element of Christian cosmology (the Christian view of the universe), especially in Western contexts that have some issues believing in the spiritual elements of our reality. But in the biblical text and in spiritual experience, many, particularly in Charismatic spaces, have highlighted the importance of recognizing the presence and activity of evil spirits and forces. For many Christians around the world, demonic powers do exist and have some influence – though we cannot always say precisely how – on our lives and experiences.

But demons also get a hard time, in my opinion. Since what precisely they are is quite vague and undefined, this leaves them open to being blamed for things that may well have nothing to do with them. The person caught out for having multiple affairs with people in their congregation blames the devil or demons for leading them astray, rather than owning their own lack of self-control. In that case, I say, leave the demons alone! So often, we as human beings struggle to own the parts of ourselves that we know would not be accepted by others, those parts of ourselves that conjure up shame. And so we ascribe them to evil forces. Where our lust is out of control to the point that we have no ability to manage our sexual appetites and thus are caught in compromising situations, we would prefer to blame a demon rather than admit it is part of us. We do not want to admit it to others, but we cannot even admit it to ourselves. Therefore the demons are held responsible for the kinds of reckless or hateful action that a person has chosen to take.

Discernment can be a simple matter of exploring what God might be desiring or saying. It might also be about examining whose voice is having influence: maybe God, maybe an evil force, but it might also just be me, or my socialization, or the perspectives I have inherited that are being outworked. It might be that this person who has abused their power has been influenced in some way by demons, but it may be them and their desires being manifested. They may have said something violent to you, embarrassed or shamed you, and this is definitely consistent with demonic activity. But did the devil make her do it? This might seem trivial but it has a huge impact on how we then respond to what has happened. Does a demon need to be prayed away? Maybe. Does this person need to be reported to the relevant authorities? Without a doubt.

Discernment and church communities

This whole book is an exercise in naming what we need to look out for in terms of the dynamics of power in our churches, especially around those designated the role of 'leader'. And lots has been written on what to avoid so I will not reiterate much here. The green flags that help me discern where to attend or stay are shared governance and a culture of reflection, care and flexibility. I want to be in a space where there is input from various people on what is happening and how. I am not comfortable with an individual or a couple leading a church with little to no actual accountability. The sign of accountability, for me, is not the picture of the board of elders on the website, but in discovering the occasions where the 'leader' or 'leaders' have not got their own way. If there is no moment in living memory when the person or people in charge have had to lay down or delay an idea because the congregation, wider team or elders did not agree, then I question the level of accountability at work. Reflection is the mark of humility at an organizational level, and this is important to me, as it demonstrates that real care is being taken over the shepherding of God's people. Care for the well-being of those working for the church, attending it, and being served by it, is a non-negotiable for me at this point. Down times during the year for the congregation and a pastor or priest who takes holidays, and allows others to, is a huge positive in my view. So is the willingness to recognize the complexity of life, which sometimes means things need to be cancelled, rearranged or reprioritized in the life of the community, or in individual lives, is essential. Anywhere that encourages the kind of rigid loyalty that ignores the human elements of our experience is a no-go for me.

Since preaching is often an important area for reflection for those who are open to finding a church home, I will mention that here. For those of us in particular who have survived harmful church or Christian environments, there is much to consider in terms of the theologies communicated through preaching. This is of course what this whole book is about. What I look for is pastoral sensitivity in preaching, and an awareness that the preacher is speaking in contexts where people may have or may be experiencing abuses of power at the hands of church leaders. This should provoke a posture of humility, a holding of the space with reverence rather than pride. It means considering how certain passages or themes will sound in the ears of a congregation who – even if not personally impacted by an abuser – are hearing constant accounts of power abuse by church leaders. What stories, themes or passages should be prioritized and how should they be preached in such a context?[6]

In my own discernment, there are some questions that help me consider whether a church is a healthy space in which I might grow in faith in God, rather than in an unhelpful dependency on particular individuals. Am I being invited to look more closely to Jesus and follow the guidance of the Spirit in my own life, or to focus and look to the person on the stage? Am I being encouraged directly or indirectly to depend on the spiritual gifts of other individuals, or to cultivate my own as part of my walk with God? Is there an approach to preaching that welcomes voices and perspectives from beyond a typical white, Western, male viewpoint?

Discerning a spiritual community to belong to is also about examining the extent to which I can have a sense of community. This may not mean anything as grand as friendship; it might simply be a space you can go along to, sit quietly during a service, and receive Holy Communion if that's your thing. Perhaps it is about being in a space where someone will notice if you are not there. But it is not a space you will be imposed upon, or where you will feel pressured in any way – especially if you are recovering from an environment that has felt abusive. You may not even need someone to follow up with you, or track you down; just to notice, and welcome you back the next time you go along. That might be all that you need – sometimes we do not have the range for anything else. In my discernment, I pay attention to those who are already there and call this place home. Do I feel I could fit in here? This is not necessarily about the age or stage of the people; there can be a homely quality even where, on paper, you would think you wouldn't fit. This is the beautiful mystery of community, and the Spirit's work in forming it. I want to know that if called by God, I could fully participate in the life of the community. I want to see there are no patterns of discrimination that affect me or others, due to race, gender, sexuality, disability, accent, class or any other aspect of who we might be.

In summary, discernment is not an easy gift to embrace. It requires a consistent openness to being awakened, and even disturbed by God as we go about our lives. It rids us of our presumptions, and demands that we admit we might not know how to see someone or something. It invites us to recognize our limits and our need for divine wisdom which we might not possess. But cultivating this is essential for us individually and collectively as we live our lives as complex people, with complex people, in a complicated world. It is especially important as we deal with the legacies of abuse in the Church, and seek to heal. This requires a discernment of what has gone wrong, what must be made right, and how we might do it.

Conclusion

This has been a painful book to write because, like so many of you, I have experienced abusive power dynamics and survived them by the grace of God and with the help of those who helped me see what was happening to me or us. I am indebted to theologians, especially feminist, womanist and Black theologians, who have given me the tools to think about my experiences with a critical eye. These are not always individuals who have written books or hold posts in universities, but they have taught me, through their own reflections and theologizing, that my own life mattered enough to ask questions of God, of the Bible and of Christian tradition. I hope this book will do the same for those who read it and wonder whether God sees or cares at all about what is happening in churches across the world.

As long as we have breath, the power really is in our hands to pull down the thrones we have created, that continue to betray us and those who are most overlooked and mistreated. While we are constantly trying to fix what is failing, we might ask greater questions about whether it needs to be repaired or reimagined altogether. I think our younger generations will force us to do this whether we like it or not. While we do our best to plough through so much of this mess, they are increasingly uninterested in the communities we are offering. This is not an attitude exclusive to young people, of course – it is a chronic problem among millennials, some of whom are in their 40s.

This book will fall short, I am sure, in some ways – there are so many themes to be addressed that will need further treatment. I have hoped to look at some of the big theological ideas that play out in many of the cases of power abuse we have seen – and which surely manifest in many of those that are seen only by God. Where my language appears unhelpful or triggering, please do not feel bound to it – release whatever you discern is not for you, especially if you are recovering from experiences of power abuse yourself. I want to end with deep gratitude to survivors whose names we know and those we do not, who have shared their stories and testimonies in hopes of bringing perpetrators to justice and to prevent further harm to others. It has grieved me to write this book, though I have felt compelled to speak to those rooted in the same traditions in which I was raised. These things should not be so, and my prayer and determination is that we do what we can, where we are, to speak up with bold voices when we see harm come to even one person. This is an obvious requirement to those of us who follow the one who made it his business to care for and welcome the smallest and most vulnerable into his presence. In this, we might be counted as Christ's followers, if we are willing to frustrate the powers through our faithfulness to the one who calls us by name.

Notes

1 Diane Langberg, *Redeeming Power: Understanding Authority and Abuse in the Church* (Grand Rapids, MI: Brazos Press, 2020), p. xiii.

2 Ignatius of Loyola, 'Rules for Perceiving and Knowing in Some Manner the Different Movements which are Caused in the Soul', *The Spiritual Exercises*, fourth rule, https://sacred-texts.com/chr/seil/seil78.htm (accessed 12.12.2024).

3 Elizabeth Liebert, *The Way of Discernment: Spiritual Practices for Decision Making* (Louisville, KY: Westminster John Knox Press, 2008), p. x.

4 For an account of spiritual practices for trauma survivors, including practices that centre the body and its wisdom, see Karen O'Donnell, *Survival: Radical Spiritual Practices for Trauma Survivors* (London: SCM Press, 2024).

5 Walter Wink, *Engaging the Powers: Discernment and Resistance in a World of Domination* (Minneapolis, MN: Fortress Press, 1992), p. 84.

6 I am inspired here by the list of eight areas of church life where sensitivity is needed for survivors of abuse, which names 'Use of the Bible in Preaching, Teaching, and Worship' above all, in Toinette M. Eugene and James N. Poling, *Balm for Gilead: Pastoral Care for African American Families Experiencing Abuse* (Nashville, TN: Abingdon Press, 1998), pp. 158–9, 164.

Bibliography

Aquinas, Thomas, Richard J. Regan (trans.), *The Power of God*, Oxford: Oxford University Press, 2012.
Barringer, Laura and Scot McKnight, *A Church Called Tov: Forming a Goodness Culture that Resists Abuses of Power and Promotes Healing*, Carol Stream, IL: Tyndale House Publishers, 2020.
Barth, Karl, *Dogmatics in Outline*, London: SCM Press, 1949.
BBC, *Catch Her if you Can*, BBC, https://www.bbc.co.uk/programmes/p08vwr8y (accessed 3.07.2024).
BBC News, 'SPAC Nation: No Criminal Probe into Evangelical Church', *BBC News*, 11 February 2020, https://www.bbc.co.uk/news/uk-england-london-51459741 (accessed 4.07.2024).
BBC News, 'SPAC Nation: London Church Wound up over Financial Mismanagement', *BBC News*, 17 June 2022, https://www.bbc.co.uk/news/uk-england-london-61844094 (accessed 3.07.2024).
BBC Panorama, 'Conned by my Church', https://www.bbc.co.uk/programmes/m000cfr5 (accessed 3.07.2024).
Beaty, Katelyn, *Celebrities for Jesus: How Personas, Platforms and Profits are Hurting the Church*, Grand Rapids, MI: Brazos Press, 2022.
Berry, Jan, 'A Safe Space for Healing: Boundaries, Power and Vulnerability in Pastoral Care', *Theology and Sexuality Journal*, 20:3 (2015), pp. 203–13.
Billy Graham Evangelistic Association, 'What's the Billy Graham Rule?', *Billy Graham*, https://billygraham.org/story/the-modesto-manifesto-a-declaration-of-biblical-integrity/ (accessed 28.11.2024).
Brock, Rita Nakashima, *Journeys by Heart: A Christology of Erotic Power*, New York: Crossroad, 1988.
Brown, Brené, 'The Power of Vulnerability', TED Talk, *YouTube*, 3 January 2011, https://www.youtube.com/watch?v=iCvmsMzlF70&t=217s (accessed 25.06.2024).
Catch the Fire Toronto, 'E/F: Insecurity (Mike Pilavachi at the School of Ministry) Mike Pilavachi', 16 September 2012, *YouTube*, https://www.youtube.com/watch?v=PbxA5YO201E (accessed 23.05.2024).

BIBLIOGRAPHY

Channel 4 News, 'Archbishop Apologises for Historic "Abuse": The Full Story', *Channel 4*, 2 February 2017, https://www.channel4.com/news/archbishop-apologises-for-historic-abuse-the-full-story (accessed 4.06.2024).

Channel 4 News, 'Police Investigate Alleged "Brutal Lashings" by Christian Leader', *Channel 4*, 2 February 2017, https://www.channel4.com/news/police-investigate-alleged-brutal-lashings-by-christian-leader (accessed 4.06.2024).

Channel 4 News, 'Christian Lawyer who "Beat Boys" was Charged over Zimbabwe Death', *Channel 4*, 3 February 2017, https://www.channel4.com/news/christian-lawyer-who-beat-boys-was-charged-over-zimbabwe-death (accessed 4.06.2024).

The Charity Commission, 'Charity Regulator Opens Inquiry into SPAC Nation', *Gov.uk*, 13 December 2019, https://www.gov.uk/government/news/charity-regulator-opens-inquiry-into-spac-nation (accessed 4.07.2024).

The Church of England, 'Concerns Substantiated in Mike Pilavachi Investigation', *Church of England*, 6 September 2023, https://www.churchofengland.org/media/press-releases/concerns-substantiated-mike-pilavachi-investigation (accessed 11.12.2024).

Coakley, Sarah, *Powers and Submissions: Spirituality, Philosophy and Gender*, Oxford: Blackwell Publishing, 2006.

Collins, Natalie, *God Loves Women* blog, https://mrsglw.wordpress.com/ (accessed 3.12.2024).

Collins, Natalie, 'Needs Light', *X*, https://x.com/needs_light (accessed 3.12.2024).

Crouch, Andy, *Playing God – Redeeming the Gift of Power*, Downer's Grove, IL: IVP, 2013.

Dawson, Rosie, '"Good and Godly Man" Ravi Zacharias Sexually Abused Women', *Religion Media Centre*, 15 February 2021, https://religionmediacentre.org.uk/news/good-and-godly-man-ravi-zacharias-sexually-abused-women/ (accessed 11.12.2024).

DeGroat, Chuck, *When Narcissism Comes to Church: Healing Your Community from Emotional and Spiritual Abuse*, Downer's Grove, IL: IVP, 2020.

Eugene, Toinette M. and James N. Poling, *Balm for Gilead: Pastoral Care for African American Families Experiencing Abuse*, Nashville, TN: Abingdon Press, 1998.

Goggin, Jamin and Kyle Strobel, *The Way of the Dragon or the Way of the Lamb: Searching for Jesus' Path of Power in a Church that Has Abandoned It*, Nashville, TN: Nelson Books, 2017.

Graystone, Andrew, *Bleeding for Jesus: John Smyth and the Cult of the Iwerne Camps*, London: Darton, Longman and Todd, 2021.

Hanson Woodruff, Kelsey, 'A Calculated Attack on Clergy Abuse: Challenging Patriarchal Power at Willow Creek Community Church', *Theology & Sexuality*, 30:1 (2024), pp. 32–49.

Harvey, Nicholas Peter and Linda Woodhead, *Unknowing God: Toward a Post-Abusive Theology*, Eugene, OR: Cascade Books, 2022.

Honeysett, Marcus, *Powerful Leaders: When Church Leadership Goes Wrong and How to Prevent It*, London: IVP, 2022.

House of Commons, UK Parliament, HC Deb (Wednesday 8th January 2020), Vol. 669, https://hansard.parliament.uk/Commons/2020-01-08/debates/04DE1B71-C7FD-46EE-BDC5-B11182AD9BF5/SPAC Nation (accessed 4.07.2024).

Ignatius of Loyola, *The Spiritual Exercises*, https://sacred-texts.com/chr/seil/seil78.htm (accessed 12.12.2024).

Inside Croydon, 'Founder of "Church of Bling" to be Deported as Illegal Immigrant', *Inside Croydon*, 4 December 2024, https://insidecroydon.com/2024/12/04/founder-of-church-of-bling-to-be-deported-as-illegal-immigrant/ (accessed 5.12.2024).

Isasi-Díaz, Ada María, *Mujerista Theology: A Theology for the Twenty-First Century*, Maryknoll, NY: Orbis Books, 1996.

Jones, William R., *Is God a White Racist?: A Preamble to Black Theology*, Boston, MA: Beacon Press, 1998.

KoinoniaFCCBC, 'Final Lesson on Jesus and Power – Rev Dr JoAnne Marie Terrell 2-23-2014', *YouTube*, 25 February 2014, https://www.youtube.com/watch?v=gL_t1mooqgo (accessed 18.06.2024).

Kruger, Michael J., *Bully Pulpit: Confronting the Problem of Spiritual Abuse in the Church*, Grand Rapids, MI: Zondervan, 2022.

Langberg, Diane, *Redeeming Power: Understanding Authority and Abuse in the Church*, Grand Rapids, MI: Brazos Press, 2020.

L'Arche International, 'Summary Report', 22 February 2020, https://www.larche.org/wp-content/uploads/documents/10181/2539004/Inquiry-Summary_Report-Final-2020_02_22-EN.pdf (accessed 5.08.2024).

L'Arche Study Commission, 'Control and Abuse Investigation on Thomas Philippe, Jean Vanier and L'Arche (1950–2019)', https://commissiondetude-jeanvanier.org/commissiondetudeindependante2023-empriseetabus/wp-content/uploads/2023/01/Report_Control-and-Abuse_EN.pdf (accessed 5.08.2024).

Lewis-Anthony, Justin, *You are the Messiah and I Should Know: Why Leadership is a Myth (and Probably a Heresy)*, London: Bloomsbury, 2013.

Liebert, Elizabeth, *The Way of Discernment: Spiritual Practices for Decision Making*, Louisville, KY: Westminster John Knox Press, 2008.

BIBLIOGRAPHY

Makin, Keith, 'Independent Learning Lessons Review – John Smyth QC (October 2024)', https://www.churchofengland.org/sites/default/files/2024-11/independent-learning-lessons-review-john-smyth-qc-november-2024.pdf (accessed 14.11.2024).

Moss III, Otis, *Dancing in the Darkness: Spiritual Lessons for Turbulent Times*, New York, NY: Simon and Schuster, 2023.

Mullen, Wade, *Something's Not Right: Decoding the Hidden Tactics of Abuse and Freeing Yourself from Its Power*, Carol Stream, IL: Tyndale Momentum, 2020.

Nyoka, Shingai and Lucy Fleming, 'I Blame the Church for my Brother's Death, Says Zimbabwean Sister of UK Child Abuser's Victim', *BBC News*, 14 November 2024, https://www.bbc.co.uk/news/articles/c62lr331lkzo (accessed 21.02.2025).

Oakley, Lisa and Justin Humphreys, *Escaping the Maze of Spiritual Abuse: Creating Healthy Christian Cultures*, London: SPCK, 2019.

Oakley, Lisa and Kathryn Kinmond, *Breaking the Silence on Spiritual Abuse*, London: Palgrave Macmillan, 2013.

O'Donnell, Karen, *Survival: Radical Spiritual Practices for Trauma Survivors*, London: SCM Press, 2024.

Orphanopoulos, Carolina Montero, 'Vulnerability, Ecclesial Abuse, and "Vulnerable Adults"', in Daniel J. Fleming, James F. Keenan SJ and Hans Zollner SJ (eds), *Doing Theology and Theological Ethics in the Face of the Abuse Crisis*, Eugene, OR: Wipf & Stock, 2023, pp. 26–39.

Overthinking Christian Blog, 'Church Abuse, Non-Disclosure Agreements, and the Billy Graham Rule: An Interview with Laura Barringer', *Overthinking Christian*, https://overthinkingchristian.com/2021/05/26/church-abuse-non-disclosure-agreements-and-the-billy-graham-rule-an-interview-with-laura-barringer/ (accessed 11.12.2024).

Phillips, Noel, 'The Church where Drugs and Knives are Left at the Altar', *BBC News*, 1 February 2018, https://www.bbc.co.uk/news/uk-42887653 (accessed 3.07.2024).

Poling, James N., *The Abuse of Power: A Theological Problem*, Nashville, TN: Abingdon Press, 1991.

Pugh, Ben, *Atonement Theories: A Way Through the Maze*, Eugene, OR: Cascade Books, 2014.

Reaves, Jayme R., David Tombs and Rocío Figueroa, eds, *When Did We See You Naked? Jesus as a Victim of Sexual Abuse*, London: SCM Press, 2021.

Redman, Matt and Beth, 'Let There Be Light', *YouTube*, https://www.youtube.com/watch?v=YVZkgdt32u8&t=36s (accessed 3.12.2024).

Santoro, Vic, Instagram, @VicSantoro (accessed 3.07.2024).

Scolding, Fiona (KC) and Ben Fullbrook, 'Independent Review into Soul Survivor', 26 September 2024, https://www.soulsurvivorwatford.co.uk/outcome (accessed 3.12.2024).

Soul Survivor, 'Launch of Independent Review', 21 November 2023, https://www.soulsurvivorwatford.co.uk/latestupdates (accessed 10.12.2024).

Soul Survivors podcast, 'Episode 3: The Open Secret', *Premier Christianity*, https://www.premier.plus/soul-survivors/podcasts/soul-survivors/episode-3-the-open-secret (accessed 3.12.2024).

Stone, Selina, *'If It Wasn't for God': A Report on the Wellbeing of Global Majority Heritage Clergy in the Church of England*, London: The Church of England, 2022, https://www.churchofengland.org/sites/default/files/2022-10/focussed-study-3-gmh-clergy-wellbeing.pdf (accessed 11.12.2024).

Terrell, JoAnne Marie, *Power in the Blood? The Cross in African American Experience*, Eugene, OR: Wipf & Stock, 1998.

Tombs, David, *The Crucifixion of Jesus: Torture, Sexual Abuse, and the Scandal of the Cross*, Oxford: Taylor & Francis Group, 2022.

Vanier, Jean, *Drawn into the Mystery of Jesus through the Gospel of John*, London: Darton, Longman and Todd, 2004.

Walsh, J.P.M., *The Mighty from Their Thrones: Power in the Biblical Tradition*, Philadelphia, PA: Fortress Press, 1987.

White, Nadine and Emma Youle, 'SPAC Nation: Allegations of Safeguarding Abuses in "Trap Houses" Linked to Controversial Church', *HuffPost*, 9 November 2019, https://www.huffingtonpost.co.uk/entry/spac-nation-scandal-safeguarding_uk_5dc5a907e4b-00927b2329c3c (accessed 3.07.2024).

——— 'SPAC Nation: Rogue Pastors Accused of Pressuring Youth to Donate Blood for Money for Church Funds', *HuffPost*, 11 December 2019, https://www.huffingtonpost.co.uk/entry/spac-nation-sell-blood-for-money_uk_5def9bb8e4b07f6835b958f5 (accessed 3.07.2024).

——— 'SPAC Nation: What We Know about Church whose Members are Accused of Fraud and Abuse', *HuffPost*, 16 December 2019, https://www.huffingtonpost.co.uk/entry/spac-nation-fraud-abuse-panorama_uk_5df6e471e4b03aed50f0650b (accessed 3.07.2024).

Williams, Delores, *Sisters in the Wilderness: The Challenge of Womanist God-Talk*, New York, NY: Orbis Books, 1993.

Wink, Walter, *Engaging the Powers: Discernment and Resistance in a World of Domination*, Minneapolis, MN: Fortress Press, 1992.

Wright, N.T. and Michael F. Bird, *Jesus and the Powers: Christian Political Witness in an Age of Totalitarian Terror and Dysfunctional Democracies*, London: SPCK, 2024.

Index of Names and Subjects

atonement 13, 92–3, 95–7, 99, 100, 101, 102–5, 106

Barth, Karl (*Dogmatics in Outline*) 56
Beaty, Katelyn (*Celebrities for Jesus*) 2, 58, 60
Bible *see also* Scripture
  in abuse/violence 5–7, 29–30, 65, 68–9, 94–5, 105, 119–22
  discernment in 136–8
  and ethics 11, 91, 105
  and hermeneutics 36, 82, 102, 104–5,
  and justice 43–6
  and survival 104–5, 133
boundaries 7, 30, 44–5, 88, 123–4, 125–8
Brown, Brené ('The Power of Vulnerability' TED Talk) 13, 109–10

Christology *see also* Jesus Christ
  atonement and the cross 90–3, 95, 99–105
  and ethics 11, 44, 66–9
  imitation of Christ 6, 115–17
  and power 6–7, 113–14, 125, 127–8
  prayer for unity 83–9
  principalities and powers 75, 78–9

church
  creating healthy culture 29, 149–51
  discernment 134–6, 138–147
  as imitators/the body of Christ 115–17
  internal conflict 77–89,
  as opposed to the world 73–7, 80–3
class 24n6 and 31, 48, 60–4, 66, 97, 139
Collins, Natalie (*God Loves Women* blog) 50
cross, crucifixion 88, 90–2, 95, 100, 101, 102–3, 105, 138

demonic powers 147–9
dignity 5, 18, 21, 51, 97, 106, 123
discernment 11, 13, 29, 74, 92, 102, 131–51

Evangelicalism, Evangelical world, communities 1, 2, 7, 31, 90, 91, 93, 96, 111, 112, 117, 124

faith 4, 5, 8, 33, 35, 46, 53, 67, 70, 75, 78, 84, 90, 91, 95, 97, 100, 102, 110, 115, 135, 140, 145, 147, 150
  community of 13, 24, 113, 136
  lost vii, 1

financial abuse 61–6, 69–70
money and power 66–70

gender 5, 20, 21, 23, 24–5, 33, 47, 92, 100, 111–12, 119–21, 151
Graystone, Andrew (*Bleeding for Jesus: John Smyth and the Cult of the Iwerne Camps*) 94, 95, 96–7

Harvey, Nicholas Peter and Woodhead, Linda (*Unknowing God*) 2, 31
Holy Spirit
 and discernment 137, 138, 139
 as divine breath, power 20–2
 and Incarnation 113, 135
 presence and work of 46, 57, 79–80, 83, 84, 87, 115

Ignatius of Loyola (*Spiritual Exercises*) 140–1

Jesus Christ *see also* Christology 6, 11, 13, 14n10, 25, 44, 45, 57, 66, 67–70, 78, 79, 81–2, 83, 84, 86, 88, 89, 90–2, 100, 101, 103, 105, 106, 114, 115–17, 120–3, 125, 127–8, 138, 150

Kinmond, Kathryn *see also* Oakley, Lisa 29
kin-dom 5, 14n10

Langberg, Diane (*Redeeming Power*) 2, 19, 23, 110, 131
leadership
 bias 27
 leaders as vulnerable to abuse 24

servant leadership 16–17, 25–6, 58–9, 113–17
silence of, 50–1
LGBTQIA+ experience 24–5

Mary, mother of Jesus 91, 113, 120
Moss III, Revd Otis (*Dancing in the Darkness*) 77–8

Oakley, Lisa 3, 28–9, 65
 and Humphreys, Justin (*Escaping the Maze of Spiritual Abuse*) 18, 24, 28–9, 34

Panorama ('Conned by my Church') 62
parable(s) 12, 44, 80, 82–3
 of the Tares (Matt. 13.24–30), 80–1
Pilavachi, Mike 36–43, 50–1
power
 definition
 as divine breath 18–22
 as social/political 23–8
 and personality 33–4, 124, 138–9
 and politics 5, 22, 27, 75–9, 146–7
prayer
 and abuse/abusers 8, 46–7, 62–3, 122
 and power 54, 75, 78, 84, 88, 134
preaching 29, 35–42, 47–8, 54, 77, 86, 92, 99, 134, 149–50

race 24, 27, 47, 74, 99–102, 142
Redman, Beth and Matt 50–1
righteousness 3, 66, 83, 115, 108n7

INDEX OF NAMES AND SUBJECTS

Scripture *see also* Bible 19, 29, 36, 46, 64, 67, 82, 120, 134
  misuse of 30, 68, 69, 119
The Secrets of Hillsong (documentary) 50, 52n15, 129n9
silence
  as bestowing power 24
  discernment 135, 143
  leaders 50–1
  silencing of victim-survivors 85–6, 30, 34, 48–9, 86
Smyth, John 93–9,
social justice and power 3–4, 20, 22, 23–8, 112, 126, 151
SPAC Nation 60–4, 66, 70
speech
  about abuse 49–51, 86
  as bestowing power 27, 43–7, 58–9, 133
  divine 46, 125, 135
  in place of God 33–4,
spiritual abuse, definition 29–30
spirituality
  charismatic 57–8, 124, 134, 138–9, 147–8.
  contemplative (Ignatian) 140–1
  pentecostal 46–7, 54, 78, 124, 138–40
  spiritual parenthood 94–5, 96, 122–3
Stibbe, Mark *see also* Smyth, John 95, 104, 105

Terrell, JoAnne Marie 93, 102–5, 109
theology, theologies 3, 6, 8, 11, 16, 17, 25, 30, 33, 43, 53, 54, 74, 76, 77, 78, 95, 102, 106, 119, 120, 122, 124, 125, 131, 141, 144, 150
  and abuse 2, 18, 28, 29, 30–1, 38, 48, 93, 94, 96, 131–2, 144
  of disability 123
  Evangelical 96, 100
  of power 3, 7, 15, 16, 19, 20, 36
  of suffering, theodicy 13, 95, 97, 99, 103
  womanist 13, 99

unity 83–9

Vanier, John 117–24
violence *see also* suffering
  in the Bible 5–7
  colonial 76
  and the cross/atonement 90–3, 99–105
vocation 11, 46, 77, 87, 132, 145
vulnerability, definition 109–13

Walsh, James P. M. (*The Mighty from their Thrones*) 43–4
Williams, Delores (*Sisters in the Wilderness*) *see also* cross, atonement 93, 100–2, 103–4, 105
Wink, Walter (*Engaging the Powers*) 146–7
Wright, N. T. and Bird, Michael F. (*Jesus and the Powers*) 75–6, 78–9

young people 37, 42–3, 60–6, 69, 93–9, 134, 152

www.ingramcontent.com/pod-product-compliance
Lightning Source LLC
Chambersburg PA
CBHW022014290426
44109CB00015B/1170